Return to the Future
By
Sigrid Undset

Translated from the Norwegian by
Henriette C. K. Naeseth

Scandinavian Marketplace
Hastings, Minnesota

First Scandinavian Marketplace Edition,
October 2001

Contents

Norway, Spring 1940

At the outskirts of almost all the cultivated land in Norway there lie great heaps of stones, which have been broken up on the fields and carried there. The first men who cleared the soil and settled here laid the under layers, – they are sunk down in the subsoil, overgrown with moss and gray with lichen. The topmost layer of smooth light stones was picked up and carted here after last year's plowing. These heaps are Norway's proudest memorials of ancient times. They are silent witnesses of our right to this land which our forefathers for more than two thousand years have toiled to conquer so that homes for man could be built on the steep sides of the valleys along the rivers, on rocky slopes and in forests, under precipitous mountains and overhanging glaciers. Here our race has wrested for itself a meager livelihood, combating rock slides and snow slides and floods, combating wild animals, and a climate that offers us nine months of winter and sometimes not even three months of the summer that makes our country a heaven on earth as long as it lasts – for in bad years frost might come as early as August, so the corn rotted unripened on the fields, and afterward the snow lay on the land until Midsummer

Eve of the next year, so it was late summer before the new seed could come into the ground.

We had our long coast, we had the uncounted riches of the sea to gather. But, God knows, even these we could not scoop up without endless toil and drudgery, and the loss of hundreds of thousands of lives. If any people in the world owns its land with honor and right, has conquered it, not from other people, but in obedience to the Creator's stern commandment that man shall eat his bread in the sweat of his brow, it is we Norwegians who call Norway our country.

Easier times came to us also, little by little. Modern agricultural science has helped us, so now we escape at least the "black years" (those years of which the old people tell, when men ground meal of bark and moss for bread, and bands of beggars roamed the country roads, until the weakest fell and died along the ditches. After it became common to raise potatoes in Norway, no one in our country, to be sure, has downright starved to death until now. Steam and motors gave our merchant marine – third largest in the world – opportunities for more extensive navigation with smaller loss of human life. Our fisheries were beginning to change from their ancient ways to modern, more scientific methods. A net of good roads and railways linked the rural districts of our long, loosely joined country – it is farther from Oslo to the North Cape than it is from Oslo to Rome. But automobile traffic had to some degree done away with the great distances between valley and valley, between town and town. Norway is an expensive country in which to build roads and railroads, but we built undaunted. We opened and with natural pride we dedicated, the modern communication lines which we ourselves were forced to destroy last spring, when we blasted our bridges, dynamited tunnels, and barricaded ourselves in mountain passes, while we tried to delay the entry of an army of marauders, who came to live where they have not built, to reap where they have not sown, to rule over a people they have never served. But it is one of the basic concepts in the Norwegian sense of what is just and right that he who shall command and rule among us must have proved that he is worthy by first having been a good servant.

We Norwegians had become a peaceful people. For this our historic position is responsible, and we should not take the credit ourselves. But the country we own lies on the far edge of Europe, it is stretched out to a disproportionate length, and only ten per cent of Norway's surface is suited to cultivation; the rest is barren gray mountain – in the west and north, wild mountain ranges with peaks and pinnacles; toward the east, upland moors, with bogs and waters, lying above the timber line, naked to storms and winter weather most of the year. And we are only about three million people – about as many as live in Brooklyn – to work and administer this country from which it is so difficult and heavy a task to win a living. No wonder we have always used our strength to save precious human lives rather than to destroy lives. Heroic deeds on sea and land to rescue men in peril of death have, thanks to God, always been daily happenings in Norway, but crimes of violence have been rarer than in any other country in Europe, and they roused our terror and abhorrence; in Norway every small murder became a topic of talk among the people for years. And if we captured one or another of our murderers he could be certain of decent treatment – of examination by psychiatrists, a conscientious lawyer, and, if he were sentenced, not too severe imprisonment. In the fifty-eight years I have lived no death sentence has been executed in Norway. The last capital punishment occurred when my father was a young boy, and when he told of it, we listened with shuddering excitement. But somehow we could not really believe it was true.

2

It was our misfortune and our stupidity that somehow we could not believe that war, either, was true. War was the kind of thing that happened in other parts of the world, we knew that, of course; but how many of us had ever seriously believed that it could happen in Norway? Finland's fight for life first awakened some of us to a more nearly realistic view of that world which we tried to keep away from our life by our policy of neutrality. But not enough of us, and too few of those who, first and foremost, should have been awake.

The German invaders broke into a country which was entirely unprepared. That the Germans here – as in all the countries they have attacked – afterward have found the inevitable documents proving that their exploit was justified self-defense is another matter.

Feine Leute haben feine Sachen,
und was sie nicht haben lassen sie sich machen,[1]

Said a German reader I had as a child.

Saturday, the 7th of April, I was in Oslo and lectured before the student society. On Sunday my two sons and I were to eat dinner at the home of my sister and brother-in-law – a late dinner because the boys were out of town somewhere or other, where the young Norwegian volunteers were drilling. Conscription in some form Norway has had since the period of the sagas. But the period of compulsory military service established by our most recent military regulations was unsatisfactorily short. And in the winter of 1939-40 quite a large number of young men participated in volunteer military drills. In spite of everything there were not so few who quite reasonably *knew* we had no guarantee that we could keep ourselves out of this

[1] Fine people have fine things,
   And what they do not have they have made to order.

World War also, although most people hardly believed seriously that we would be drawn in. My older son had lived in England for four years and had come home in August, having completed his training as a British engineer. He was very familiar with the English system of territorial auxiliary troops, – a number of his friends there were "Terries." He had, however, no overwhelming confidence in the worth of these "Territorials." But at home at Lillehammer he offered to act as instructor for the volunteer target practice; he was an officer in the reserves. And when he got a position in Oslo a week or two before war broke out, he continued the same work there in his free time. My younger son, who was under the age of military service, was studying in Oslo and had registered for the military training, which had just been arranged for the students of the University.

In the evening my sister and I went to a musical soirée, which was given by Finnish artists as a benefit for Finnish aid. It was still the fate of Finland that dominated our thoughts and actions. Since the Finns themselves, after the bitter peace, at once took up the desperately difficult tasks confronting them, the rebuilding of their ravaged country and the provision of homes and livelihood for ninety-five per cent of the population in the provinces which they had to surrender to Russia, we in the other Scandinavian countries also would continue our work for Finnish aid as energetically as we could.

I remember two things from that soirée: a Finnish actress who recited two of the psalms of David. I have forgotten her name. That she scintillated talent is not remarkable; Finns have theatrical talents in abundance also. She stood, a small figure, dressed in black, a little stooped, and read the age-old verses as if she talked alone to her Lord and God, Jehovah, who has denounced the unrighteous of the earth; with burning passion she demanded justice for her people, revenge against the men of violence. – And a Norwegian authoress who came sailing in with some German-looking persons. She was so radiant I had to think of a Norwegian folk saying: "To smile like a viper in a silver dish." For years this lady had battled heroically to attain a position in Norwegian literary circles, with a colossal energy and a diminutive talent. And at last she had gained the sought-for position – in Germany. She was, with the exception of Knut Hamsun, the only Norwegian author who unwinkingly sided with Nazi Germany.

Immense headlines in the Monday morning papers expressed Norwegian indignation over the new English violation of our neutrality. England had mined the Norwegian waters in three places. Just as during the *Altmark* affair some months before, our indignation was much greater – or at least more openly voiced – at a British violation of our neutrality than at the Germans' constant bombing of our merchant vessels and their murder of our sailors, whom they machine-gunned in the lifeboats. But we really had never expected anything else of the Germans. Of the English we expected that they would at least not openly encroach upon our rights. And we assumed that it was not entirely useless to protest to England.

Everyone believed that the mines were laid to prevent the Germans from transporting Swedish ore from Narvik. We had no idea that the German invasion troops were already on their way to Norway and Denmark – that for months such an invasion had been in preparation, and presumably had been planned in the minutest detail even before the outbreak of the war. When the evening papers brought news that a German fleet of more than a hundred ships of different types was headed northward through the Danish sounds, only a very few of us believed it meant anything except that the great sea fight in the North Sea, which rumor had been busy with all winter, at last was to become a reality.

I had gone to bed at my hotel – a small, somewhat old-fashioned hotel, where I have stayed when in Oslo since the poorest days of my youth – but was lying there reading when the sirens sounded at half past twelve. And with the news of the German fleet fresh in my mind I really did think for a moment: "Does it mean that something is happening?" Still I felt that I was behaving almost ridiculously when I got up, put on stockings and shoes, and my fur coat over my nightgown. When I came out in the corridor there was nobody in sight.

The only sign of anything unusual was the night porter was not at his desk and there was no elevator service. But such things had happened before at this hotel. So I walked down all the stairs to the main entrance.

The street lights and neon signs were moderately bright, as usual (the lights were never bright in that part of Oslo). And some young girls and boys who stood in the doorway shook their heads – they did not know what the sirens meant. Little by little more of the hotel guests came sauntering down. The watchman in the courtyard was said to have the key to a shelter which was said to have been arranged in the cellar. But it was impossible to get hold of him. At last one of the bellboys came and showed us down a cellar stairway which led to a room under a small theater in the block. And there we stood, in completely darkness, and froze, and smoked cigarettes, and joked and guessed at what the alarm could mean – practice or something serious? Perhaps this sea fight was going on outside Ferder, and some planes had come over Norwegian territory. When a lieutenant in the Air Corps, a mere youngster, gave this theory all the weight of his authority the majority agreed that this was probably right. None of us dreamed of a German landing in Norway.

When we had stood there an hour or two we heard the all-clear signal, and we went up and to bed again. But in a short time the alarm sounded once more. This time nobody bothered to go to the cellar.

We sat in the lobby, and the manageress and some of the guests provided food and drinks. At about the time when one of the bellboys came in with a pile of fresh handbills which told of the bombing of the two airports at Oslo, Fornebu and Kjeller, and fighting between the coast fortifications in the Oslo fjord and German battleships, we saw the first bomber. In the gray dawn it flew over the square outside the hotel so low that we could see the national emblem, the black and white Maltese cross, and the people in the plane. More came at once. And in every direction shots cracked and sputtered; the German fliers are said to have let the machine-guns play, and all that Oslo possessed of anti-aircraft guns answered. Unfortunately without bothering the Germans in the least.

When I walked up to the eight o'clock mass at St. Olav's Church, the planes were cruising back and forth over the city. In the streets people were going to their work as usual. They looked a little puzzled: no one had any idea of what bombing is like, that was clear. When the planes came directly over our heads we stepped into a shop door or a gateway. But in the church the sisters and schoolchildren were absent – the whole school had been evacuated. So Monsignor was alone at the altar, without choirboys. And we were only five elderly women at the mass. It proceeded to the accompaniment of shooting and the drone of motors.

I managed to get hold of an automobile and

drove to the concern where Anders, my older son, worked. They had not seen him. I drove to his room – rang and rang, but nobody answered. Back to the hotel – to tell the truth, I was suddenly aware of being hungry. In the lobby I met my younger son, Hans. Outside the city, where he lived, they had slept calmly all night – noticed nothing of air alarms or invasion. I decreed that he was to go home with me to Lillehammer – that is, if the trains were running.

I had one more errand to do in town. A private automobile picked us up; the driver wore a white armband to show that he was one of the volunteer workers. While we drove we heard an impromptu church service over the radio. They sang *A Mighty Fortress is Our God*. When they came to the line: "Our own power is without worth," Hans broke into laughter: "God knows that is the truth." It was not quite so bad as that, it became clear later. We fought back pretty hard – withstood the German rapacity longer than any of the other victims, except England.

There was nobody at the legation where I had an errand. It was here we learned that our King and government had left Oslo, and that the Minister concerned had gone with the government to which she was accredited. It does no harm now if I say that it was Mrs. Florence Borden Harriman, who in Norway's fateful hour so definitely took her stand with all which represented law and justice and order in Norway that her place in the hearts of all faithful

Norwegians is assured as long as April 9 is remembered in Norway.

Back to the hotel. I proposed that we had better go down to the East Station and see if we could get a train north to Lillehammer. For one thing, I had three small Finnish children at home at Bjerkebaek, evacuated from one of the most severely bombed districts of Finland.

Just as we were going to get into the car, Anders came, stooped under his load of knapsack, gun, and so on. He had been down and reported to his division, the Automobile Corps, but there he had been told that it was impossible to mobilize any of the units which were to have been set up in Oslo. He could not go with us, he probably had to help some other young boys to get out of town to one of the places where our troops could assemble. He thought he could manage to get home to Lillehammer during the night, so he could report for duty at Jörstadmoen, outside town. All the young men for whom it was at all possible wanted to get to the army; they were fully determined to fight. Unmobilized, inadequately armed, and unprepared, but stubbornly furious at the German outrage, they wanted to do what could be done, at least to delay and make difficult the bandit army's entry into our country.

Down at the East Station people stood as closely packed as herrings in a barrel. But I saw no sign of panic. Foreign correspondents who are used to dealing with people who do not, like the

Norwegians, consider it indecent to reveal one's feelings could undoubtedly easily get the impression that we were indifferent to what happened to us and to our country. Thus the many young boys expressed their hope that if they were to fall they might at least get a chance to "salt down" as many Germans as possible first with considerably less excitement than I have seen these same boys show in talking over yesterday's bridge party.

The morning train to Lillehammer was not more than an hour late. It was packed full; Hans and I sat on our trunks in the aisle. There were not so few boys in uniform – young men who had tried in vain to find their divisions in Oslo. Several in Finnish uniforms – they had been over there and fought as volunteers. Some Jews and German-speaking foreigners – refugees from the Hitler regime, whom our organizations, the Nansen organization for the aid of refugees and the Labor Party's aid committee, had got into Norway. That they showed themselves more nervous than we others was certainly quite natural. But we did not understand it then – we whispered a little critically about their lack of self-control.

Just as we left the station some bombs fell so close by that the train shook and lurched as if it would jump the rails. The windows seemed to swell under the air pressure, but they held. And someone remarked: "If a bomb had struck the waiting-room there might have been a beautiful blood bath here."

At Lilleström we all peered out toward the

airport at Kjeller; it was supposed to have been bombed early that morning. But we could not see anything. At Jesseim and Hauerseter, the stations nearest one of our relatively large military centers, there were crowds of soldiers. And a good many of the young men scurried to get off the train there. At all the stations were swarms of people who had come to get news of what had really happened in Oslo. At the Hamar station some of our best-known Storting[2] men were walking – the Storting had assembled in Hamar.

It was late evening when we reached Lillehammer. There the blackout took care of itself: our electric power comes from the falls outside the town, and after a rare autumn and a winter with little snow and months of unbroken frost the reservoirs were almost empty. So the electric power was shut off over the whole town at nightfall. I came home to a dark house – and there was nobody at home except the little parlor maid, who was undressing the Finnish children. My housekeeper and the garage-owner who used to drive for us had rushed off to Oslo to try to find the boys and me and bring us home to Lillehammer.

Elmi was four, Toimi three, and Eira two years old. Children of that age are creatures of habit – they were glad I had come home again and could help the maid undress them as usual. But when I heard the drone of a plane out in the half-light

2 The Norwegian parliament.

spring night, and the siren at the woolen factory began its thin cry, I decided to take the children down to the first story and make beds for them there. Elmi was standing by me having her sleeping-garment buttoned; in the dim light I saw the little girl's face: she seemed to be remembering something she did not like. She was the only one of the three children who had shown signs of nervousness when they came to me. The boy Toimi, was lying in his bed and saying something which sounded like: *"Pekka Molotovin,"* while he pointed to the window. Eira, energetic as always, protested violently against being moved downstairs and put to bed on a sofa. I had to take her on my lap to get her to sleep.

In spite of everything there was something sweet and peaceful about sitting this way in the dark and hearing the three little children breathing so quietly and healthily around me. But at the same time the thought that they had come here because they were to have a refuge from bombing and suffering and death, but now violence and bombers pursued them here, was such that at times one felt one would suffocate with rage.

At about midnight my housekeeper and the chauffeur came. We drank coffee and ate in the kitchen, by a tiny stearin light, while they told about their trip to the city. On the way down, the car had been filled with people who wanted to get to Oslo to hunt up their relatives. Just outside Oslo they had had to get out of the car and sit in a ditch while bombs fell near by. On the way back, they brought with them people from Oslo who wanted to evacuate to their relatives in the country.

A little later Anders came, hungry and thirsty, and very silent. He saw quite clearly that it was a difficult task to mobilize, after the enemy had already got a foothold in the country – and help from traitors within. How many traitors nobody knew. We had never taken seriously our native National Socialists. To ordinary healthy and normal Norwegians the whole National Socialist ideology is so alien – and at that time it was its comic aspect we chiefly saw – that we were inclined to dismiss Quisling and his *"hird"*[3] with a shrug of the shoulders, as hysterical half-men. *Now* we were inclined to believe that there were perhaps many more than we had suspected – that the little flock at whom we had laughed so much probably had behind them a much larger crowd of fortune-hunters and traitors who had the sense to keep still until their lords, the Germans, were ready to support them in Norway. There *were* some of these secret Nazis if not nearly so many as foreign countries have been inclined to believe. And instead of the smile at Quisling and the Quislingites there has arisen a white-hot hate for the Germans' errand boys. Only the contempt for them is the same. It could hardly become greater than it already was.

[3] Old Norse for a king's retinue. The word is really borrowed from Anglo-Saxon, a fact our local Nazis resented very much when they learned it from one of our most famous professors of philology.

3

I had a glimpse of Anders early the next morning as he came out of the bathroom. He had already hurried off to Jörstadmoen when I came down to breakfast. A little later he telephoned and asked Hans to bicycle over with his uniform effects. And then Hans called up from the drill grounds. He had talked to an officer in the Medical Corps who said he could use volunteers, even if they had had no previous training. So he and a friend of the same age had volunteered. Could we furnish him a sleeping-bag, find boots and clothes? About dinner-time he came home, got his things, and said: "Good-by. So long. You must not worry about me, Mother – you know we are not in danger in the Medical Corps." I had my own opinion about that, but I did not say anything. It was good, of course, that the boy could find something useful to do.

Only two days since we had believed in peace and no danger. And now my two boys – and the young sons of all my acquaintances in Lillehammer, and any number of the older men from business and offices – were in the war. Well, there was enough to do at home all the same. In our unbelievable optimism we felt almost certain that to Lillehammer the Germans would never come. Evacuees from Oslo, evacuees from Trondhjem, came to my house almost every day; they needed food and money, advice and help – and in return they told us of their experiences and all the conflicting rumors which were in circulation.

A German priest, a refugee from the Hitler regime, settled down in my house, hopefully expecting Trondjem surely to be recaptured very soon. His crime at home in Germany was that when the Jewish children were persecuted in the schools of the little Bavarian town where he was the director of the Catholic school system, he had given orders that they should be admitted to Catholic schools on the same conditions, as the other children, only to be excused from religious instruction. And he had accompanied a wealthy Jew to his grave – a Jew who in the years of want had helped needy people and institutions on a large scale, without asking whether they were Jewish, Protestant, or Catholic. And at the grave he had made a speech in commemoration of the dead man, in Hebrew.

He was undoubtedly a good man and a good priest. But the involuntary aversion to all things German was already so strong – and the priest was so essentially German. He wore on my nerves. With the most unrealistic optimism he prophesied Hitler's early downfall, delivered long lectures about Hebrew grammar, and the development of Church Latin from the last Latin vernacular, and so on. And made the same not very funny witticisms innumerable times each day.

Day in and day out the sun shone from the cloudless, serene blue heaven. In my garden the snow was melting, and the Finnish youngsters messed around in water and mud to their hearts' content; they were as wet as drowned kittens each time we had to go out and call them in because the air alarms sounded. Lillehammer had no air defenses, so the German planes flew unbothered over the town many times a day. But for the present they made no attempt to harm us; they were bombers and transport planes; most of them, we supposed, were going to Trondhjem.

And still – in spite of the planes, in spite of the motor trucks full of soldiers which drove through the streets all day long, in spite of the sentries with poised bayonets in front of all public buildings, in spite of the motorcycles with orderlies which roared through the streets – in the heavenly spring weather it was so difficult to understand that this was really the war. Every evening at nightfall my seamstress, who lived down at the station, came; she slept at my house because it lay a little outside the town limits, in a small wood, so it was supposed to be relatively safe. For that matter, it does not get very dark at night in Lillehammer in April. I went to bed half dressed, by an open window, ready to run down and warn the others if anything should happen. Outside, in the spring night, passed the steady stream of cars along the roads on both sides of Lake Mjösen. Troop transports, ammunition transports. They were not very strict about dimming their car lights. No, we were still not used to having war in our country.

The Oslo radio had been in the hands of the Germans since April 9, so nobody believed anything that was said over it. Ever since Hitler took

Czechoslovakia it had been part of youthful jargon to ask, when one doubted something that was said: "Is it true or is it German?" But our government still had two broadcasting systems, Hamar and Vigra. We knew that there was fighting everywhere along the roads which led northward to Lillehammer, and one day the Germans were so near that I was afraid to have the Finnish children in the house. We had heard the story of the bombing of Elvrom, of the many civilians who were killed in the cellars there. So I got hold of a car and drove them to a friend who lived far up in a side valley. None of us dreamed that it was to become a scene of war. Eira had already made herself at home on the lap of her new foster-mother when I said good-by to the children. And Elmi and Toimi had discovered that there were sheep and lambs on the farm, – they hardly had time to say good-by to Sigrid-Täti ("Auntie Sigrid").

Not two weeks later the family had to evacuate this farm, as motorized German troops made their way down the valley from three directions. And during the battle for the bridge down over the river Anders fell as he was bringing three machine-guns into position on the river bank.

The day after I had sent the children away I got a little more the feeling of war. During the afternoon we suddenly heard the drone of a plane, violently loud. When we looked out the window we saw it come so low, with its course right towards the house, that it looked as if it must hit the wall. For once the priest, my housekeeper, and I ran into the cellar. Immediately afterward the machine-gun fire crackled – it sounded as if it were right outside the front door. We rushed up to see what this could be; then Norwegian soldiers ran through my garden. The plane, a transport machine, had fallen in the meadow just outside my house. Down the road women and children came running; they had in all simplicity run up to look at the plane and had been seriously frightened when machine-guns had been turned on them. Outside my garden gate I met a group of ten or twelve German civilians, who seemed to follow the course of events with intense interest. They said they were refugees who lived in one of the hotels at the other end of the town. How it happened that they could be at the "scene of war" less than two minutes after the plane had landed here, it is not easy to understand.

The whole skirmish probably did not last more than three quarters of an hour. Then the German officer shot himself, and the men were taken prisoner. The Norwegian soldiers, who had not had any weapons other than their guns, looked happy, as they drove past us in the motor trucks; for most of them it was probably their first encounter. But now we knew that the war had really come here, too.

The next day I got my guest, the priest, sent over to Sweden. It was managed through the Labor Party's organization. The clerical gentleman looked happy and contented as he stood in the compartment window, between an Austrian Communist and his Lebensgefährtin, and waved farewell and until we should meet again.

In my youth I worked for ten years as a secretary in a business office. So now, when I did not have any more refugees and refugee children to look after, I telephoned to the Commandant at Lillehammer and asked if there was anything for which he could use me. He needed several censors, – all mail from the Mjösen districts was sent through Lillehammer. So I was a clerk again – walked to my work every morning, sometimes a little delayed on the way because planes passed over our heads.

I read through more than a thousand letters. It was of course, our duty to keep secret what we learned in this way. But this much I can surely say: the great majority of the letters were dominated by two feelings. That the German attack had come so unexpectedly, and seemed so meaningless, that even people who had seen their farms go up in flames, or lost a husband or son, somehow could not yet believe it was reality. And a resigned determination: since we have been forced to defend ourselves, then we would have to do what we could. We were poorly prepared – that everyone knew – but there is a Norwegian adage which says: "One must drive with the harness one has when one has nothing better." Married men often wrote to their wives: "For the children's sake, you know, even if I should fall – and I hope that will not happen – then it is better than if I should live and not be able to answer them when they get older and ask: 'What did you do, Father, when the Germans invaded Norway in 1940?' "

4

The First English troops passed through Lillehammer. They were not many, and the boys were mere youngsters – as far as I know, almost all "Territorials." Those I talked to, some Yorkshire lads, seemed, frankly speaking, more like Boy Scouts on an outing than like soldiers. Among other things, they had not suspected that it was still winter in Norway – we call it spring when the snow begins to melt. But great masses of snow still lay on the ground, and the ice on the waters had not yet commenced to break up. This also made the progress of the Germans easier – at only a few places did the Norwegians succeed in mining and breaking up the ice so some hundreds of Germans drowned.

Saturday, April 20, we heard that the English had given up the positions on Bröttum, south of Lillehammer, and we might expect the Germans to march into town during the day. I was advised to leave the town before they came. I had constantly written and spoken against Nazism and had also taken active part in the work of helping refugees from central Europe. Moreover it was said that the Germans were in the habit of taking people who had some position in the country and forcing them to speak over the radio, telling about how well the

Germans behaved, and the like, or so and so many Norwegian hostages would be shot. Supposedly it was in this way they had got a prominent representative of the Norwegian Established Church to advocate the German cause over the Oslo radio.

I had just enough time to put the most necessary things in a bag. I had no money in the house, there had been so many evacuees there who had needed help. And now the banks were closed. My housekeeper made me take a hundred crowns as a loan. With them I managed very well to Stockholm. Only at one place in Romsdal were we allowed to pay for the car which took us from Molde to the coast. Otherwise it was the same story everywhere: "We do not take pay from our countrymen now." Some added: "Soon all of us will be equally poor." There had been found on some of the fallen Germans small German-Norwegian conversation manuals. The most important section in them dealt with the requisitioning of our commodities and our cash.

A military car took me up through the valley. Everywhere along the way we passed soldiers, small supplies of ammunition, the army's automobiles. And all the time we had to keep watch for planes – automobiles were always in danger of being machine-gunned. So it was late afternoon before I came to the large farm up in the valley (it was used as a school for the young people of the district) where I planned to stop and ask about some friends, Professor Fredrik Paasche and Dr. Anders Wyller.

Fredrik Paasche, who for the last few years had laid all other work aside to serve the Nansen organization for aiding refugees, is now working outside Norway. And Anders Wyller, one of the most noble, most unselfish idealists I have met in my life, went to England with what was left of our army when we had to give up the battle for northern Norway. In London he learned that he had cancer and must die. He was flown back to Sweden, hoping to get permission to get over the border and die in Norway. But before it could be arranged – if it could have been arranged – he died in Stockholm. So I suppose it cannot harm them if I now say that we experienced the next weeks' travel adventures together.

The Norwegian radio stations at Hamar and Vigra had been silenced now, but an attempt had been made to rig up a new station in the north of the valley. And we were asked to work in the broadcasting and Norwegian press service. On Sunday Fredrik Paasche and I drove northward. In the attic above an outhouse at one of the railroad stations in the valley we made records for the radio, my manuscript lying on the washing machine of the station master's wife while I talked.

We also had an errand at Dombaas. There we saw for the first time the results of bombing; several of the small frame houses were smashed into kindling wood. At some places fires were still smoldering in the ruins. English soldiers loitered in the streets and looked into shop windows which had lost their panes. We had hardly reached the hotel – which was full of Norwegian officers – when the air alarm sounded. In Dombaas nothing like an air shelter was to be found; we had to wade through soft snow, yards deep, over a field, into a small pine wood. A kind of path had, to be sure, been trampled down in the snow to this place of refuge, but there were many hundreds of us going there, mostly soldiers in white snow-clothes, so sometimes we sank into the snow up to our waists.

It was the kind of wonderful winter-spring day that we have in Norway in April. There is a good smell from the melting snow, a fragrance of pine needles, it smells of moss and wet earth wherever a stony mound juts up out of the snow. And through the crowns of the trees whispers a sweet, soft murmur – a murmur which became audible each time the drone of the planes' motors receded a little and there was a pause in the firing. It was a little strange whenever the bombers came directly above my head and the machine-guns chattered; now and then some branches and twigs rattled down over us. For two hours I lay flat in a snowdrift between three fir trees, and a solider lying in the neighboring drift entertained me by talking about a dancing party at my home which he had attended the preceding Christmas. He was from Lillehammer, a friend of one of my sons, but what mother in these days knows any of the young people who come and dance in her house?

The Germans bombing was concentrated on the

railroad station. And the American military attaché, Captain Losey, who was standing in the entrance of one of the tunnels on Dombaas, was killed by a splinter from a bomb which fell just outside.

A soldier with his head bandaged helped me up from a hole in the snow, and we waded back to the hotel. "We can at least look the Finns in the eyes now," he said, and did not look discontented. I think he gave expression to what many young Norwegians felt. They had ardently wished to help Finland. And the rumors that Germany supposedly had threatened immediate invasion, if any of the other northern countries granted Finland official military aid they had found it difficult to believe. Now at least we understood they had not been only empty excuses.

Some of the boys expressed the pious wish that the Devil might soon take Hitler. "Pshaw, he doesn't dare," explained a boy from somewhere near Trondhjem; "he knows that then Hitler will only offer to protect Hell, and before he knows it Satan himself will be reduced to the rank of fireman in his old establishment."

5

It was announced that the English and Norwegian positions in the pass at Tretten were threatened, and a medical division arrived to set up a field hospital on the farm. We had to move up farther into the valley. We were packed into a car,

Fredrik Paasch, his wife, and two children of eight and ten, their housekeeper, and I. We drove up the valley on a military pass, stopped ten or twelve times by soldiers who were building barricades on the roads and mining the mountainsides. During the morning we reached a farm at Dovre, where relatives of the people with whom we had stayed farther down in the valley would give us shelter.

And the strongest impression from this flight through Norway, always behind our retreating lines, is this: how unspeakably beautiful this country of ours is! And how incomparably kind and helpful they were, each person we met!

At Dovre the snow on the sides of the valley had almost completely disappeared – much snow never falls in northern Gudbrandsdal; the mountains intercept the clouds. But the fields were pale and yellowish-brown in their withered grass, with not a tinge of green yet visible. And farther on, on both sides of the valley, swelled the mountain heights, dazzling white with snow, with blue shadows in the hollow between the two tops, about which an old peasant said to me once that they were exactly like a woman's two breasts.

The countryside of Dovre has been inhabited since the Stone Age, and almost all of the valley is cultivated. In the middle of the grassy slope on the sunny side is a row of stately farms with sunburnt old wooden buildings. The oldest settlements in our valleys are often built in this way because in the valley bottom along the river the frost smoke comes in the early autumn. But down along the main road and the railroad, around the stations, there has grown up a new settlement of businesses, schools, artisans' and tradesmen's houses, not to forget filling stations and garages. They lie half hidden in the thickets which grow on the sandy plains along the river. The needles of the pine trees already had their spring-like snow-washed color tone of yellow-green, and the birches were turning shiny brown and shimmering violet, for the buds were already swelling.

Every day the German planes came and bombed the station and the railroad bridge at Talleraas, though without hitting. On the whole it was surprising to see, how little they accomplished with their bombing in the country, where the population is scattered. While they were smashing our small towns into matches and setting them on fire with incendiary bombs, the entire result of the bombing at Dovre was that a poor widow's barn burned and she lost all her livestock – two cows and three goats. And outside a garage a man was killed by machine-gun fire. At least during the days I was at Dovre I had the impression that all which lived and stirred outdoors was machine-gunned from planes. We stood on the hill outside the farm where we were staying, the farm boy, an older man, and I, and watched an air battle over Dombaas, when a plane came sweeping quite low over the meadow and tried to pepper us. Fortunately the shots scattered so widely – at distances of two or three yards – that none of us was injured. But we hurried when we ran to hide in the stone stable on the farm. From time to time the Germans also hurled a load of incendiary bombs at one of the farms, so far as I know without hitting the houses anywhere. At any rate, all I ever saw was incendiary bombs left lying on the steep fields on the hillsides, spouting yellow smoke.

All the same we thought it was safest to go up to the heights during the daytime, to some small farms which lie far up under the rim of the mountains. And there we sat out on the slope and let ourselves be baked through by the spring sun, between the times we had to go into the house because of planes.

The valley lay in a Sabbath-day peace under the flood of spring sunshine, for it was impossible for people to start working in the fields. The cows stood winter-thin in the stable, the horses were requisitioned. But sheep and lambs and goats with frolicsome small kids played around the outhouses and nibbled last year's dead grass. It was this enforced idleness that was the greatest strain on the farmers' nerves – much more than the planes, which came at short intervals and disturbed the Sunday mood.

Then there was the problem of getting the farmer's youngsters in – a terrible struggle. They wanted to see; so did the Paasche children. The smallest we hauled in with main force. The next thing was to keep them from standing at the windows looking out on the valley, because every time a bomb exploded on the hill down by the station, the house trembled and quaked so we were afraid the window-panes would break. But the youngsters were wild with excitement. There the flying-machine let go the little black "turd," so the children said; then came the great shower of earth and stone and bits of trees – and then, a little later, the hollow boom as it hit the ground and exploded.

The woman of the farm treated us incessantly with coffee and rich milk, cakes and freshly baked waffles. The dairy stood idle; and if things went so badly that the Germans should come to Dovre, she would at least have had the satisfaction of serving all the best food she had in her house to countrymen. Pay – no, that was not to be thought of. "If things go right, then perhaps some time there will be something you can do for me. And if things go wrong, then I suppose we shall all be equally poor – at any rate those who are decent people," she laughed.

At the farm next to the large farm where we slept at night a band of parachute troops had been taken prisoner the week before. They were a hundred and fifty men who had barricaded themselves in the stone stable and tyrannized the whole countryside. The Norwegians brought up artillery, and after some fifty Germans had been killed, the others surrendered. The parachute troops were naturally the chief topic of conversation in the district. But what had made the strongest impression on the farmers was that the woman on the farm was certain she recognized one of the soldiers: he had come hiking to the farm one day in August the year before, had been given shelter and a little money before he went on.

It is possible that the woman was mistaken. But it is certain that great numbers of these *Wandervögel* – *Bettelvögel*[4] we called them – who tramped through Norway by the thousands summer after summer, without money, without much more baggage than the indispensable camera, got free rides in our automobiles, slept for nothing on our farms, got food from the farmers and often a little clothing or some money, returned as soldiers in the invasion army and as men who knew the country. While they drew sketches and took pictures they told of how bad conditions were in Germany – they were not allowed to take more than ten marks out of the country for traveling expenses. So the assumption was they were to live on Norwegian charity. And it did not fail them. Nobody is more clever than the Germans at complaining and asking for pity – when they do not precisely have the power to pose as *Herrenvolk*. And nobody is more quick to be moved by jeremiads than Norwegians, who are ashamed if they see anyone show overbearing ways in relations with their servants: ugh, he is an uneducated fellow; ugh, she is certainly no lady.

It is also certain that among the German soldiers were many of our old *Wienerbarn* – the German children who during the years of want after the

---

[4] Wandervögel, "Migrating Birds," members of the Nazi Youth Movement hiking clubs; Bettelvögel, "Begging Birds," beggars.

former World War were taken into Norwegian homes, fed and made fat, and brought back to health and normal childhood. And if it is true that this German way of giving thanks for hospitality, at that time at any rate, angered people in general more than almost anything else about the invasion, it has at least in an emphatic way killed the belief that there should be any particular "kinship of race" between the German people and the Norwegians. "They and we are supposed to be sort of related," said the farmers; "damned lies and bosh!"

In the dusk, when we returned to the farm, the soldiers came. They were boys who had been sent behind the front, when the English took over the defense of Kvams-Kvamsporten, the narrow mountain pass at the entrance to Kvam, Kvam parish. They were to rest for some days – many of them had fought, in action after action, from the first days of the war, when the fighting was still going on in the regions north of Oslo. And always as they fought they had to retreat, and retreat again. But none of those I talked to had lost courage. They sat in the dark kitchen while we prepared food for them, and our host brought out everything which could be used to provide them as good beds as possible. But none of them would hear of us women giving up our beds to them. So I slept every night on my spring mattress, warm and comfortable in my fur coat, and had a bad conscience because of the soldiers who were sleeping on the floors in all the rooms of the house.

One would not have known that they had been in a war – they were exactly as Norwegian young men usually are, quiet, well brought up, friendly boys. When they were asked, they would talk a little about their war experiences – low-voiced, unassuming. Only it was too bad that they had not had better equipment – and more training and more experienced leadership, although very many of the officers, and nearly all of the youngest, lieutenants and ensigns, had done as well as they could. But with only rifles and some machine-guns and a few cannon it was of course impossible in the long run to withstand the planes and tanks. That they were as good as the Germans, man for man, they knew now. And they wanted to get in the fighting again. But now they were tired, and hungry. At first they had got as much food as they could eat, for outside the large farms in the south of the country the women had stood by the wayside with five-gallon cans full of milk and coffee and pea soup, clothes-baskets of bread and butter and hard-boiled eggs. But the last days it had often been long between the times they had got anything to eat. And of sleep they had had little the whole time; usually it had been only a brief nap on the motor lorries which carried them from fight to fight.

None of them knew anything about my sons – indeed, I did not expect to find anyone who had actually met them.

Two or three of the soldiers mentioned, a little reluctantly, that it was really strange – they had seen

German boys fall in heaps before machine-gun fire; but somehow it never seemed to have any effect on them. They thought it was probably because the Germans howled and yelled and sang so horribly while they were advancing. It was almost as if they were not people – only some kind of loathsome animal whose noise one wanted to stop.

From other sources I later heard the same thing; the German howling made it impossible for the Norwegians to get it into their heads that they are people as we are. The Norwegians were as silent as the mountains when they fought.

Unbidden, the professor's young housemaid had taken command of the kitchen. And it was beautiful to see with what respect and gratitude our soldiers accepted her services, and how eager they were to help us straighten and wash up before they went on and made room for a new lot.

6

At Molde Norwegian papers were still being published, and we were advised to go there. Again it was to say good-by to strangers who had given us food and shelter, who would accept nothing from us – only wished us "luck on the journey, and may we meet again in better times."

Again we crowded together in a car and drove at night through Dombaas in ruins, through Lesja, where the snow along the road was torn up by bomb craters and the farms stood with doors splintered and windows broken, down into Romsdal. That the English entry here was more than difficult is clear: In Romsdal the west-coast nature begins, the valley is narrow and wild, with a swift river in the valley bottom and steep mountainsides – sharp peaks and black mountain chasms were silhouetted against the clear green night sky, and the green ice of the glaciers overhanging the road. It is far between places where there is room for a farm or a cluster of farms, and most of the farms are small. A single-track railroad and a country road, so narrow that at many places it is difficult for two meeting automobiles to pass, wind through the narrow mountain pass; and all the way we saw the results of the bombing of the road and the railroad. But parties of workers were busy everywhere repairing the damage done by the day's bombing, and keeping the country road from becoming quite impassable; melting snow and heavy traffic had seen to it that it was in a terrible state.

Day was dawning when the red glow of fire above the next mountain pass showed us that we were approaching Aandalsnes. Houses were burning on both sides of the street as we drove through the little town, and sooty black soldiers and civilians struggled to tear down walls which were about to fall the wrong way.

Then we were out in full spring, out by the fjord which lay bright as silk and pale blue, mirroring the last red of evening and the first pale gleams of rose before sunrise. Down over the mountainsides rushed the brooks, brimming with water, the meadow was touched with green, the soldiers wore anemones on their tunics. The first spring flowers had blossomed here by the sea.

At the farm in the arm of a fjord where we found shelter for some days, the farmer was plowing. Planes cruised over the countryside, and small gray and white dots of smoke on the light-blue sky over the mountain ridge back of the farm showed that the anti-aircraft guns at Aandalsnes had not yet given up. Occasionally a stray shell from near Aandalsnes whistled through the air over our heads. We threw ourselves flat on the ground when they came, but usually they fell into the sea below the farm. And the people in Landfjord did not let themselves be disturbed, but went about their work between the houses and out on the fjord.

"Did you manage to save any of your chairs and beds, you people?" asked the tiny girl from Aandalsnes. Her home had been burned to the ground, and her parents had not saved anything but their bare lives. "And when, moreover, a man is a glazier in a bombed town – it is certainly a pretty hard fate," said her father with gallows humor.

One evening word came that the English had given up the fight in southern Norway. They had embarked at Aandalsnes, and the Germans were supposed to be coming down through Romsdal. It meant that we had to flee farther.

The farmer and his wife who had welcomed us as

guests for four days and nights and could not do too much for us bade us good-by. The man shook hands with us: "We shall meet again." But the wife embraced us and burst into tears. It is so unlike Norwegian farm women to show their emotions that it seemed as if her tears for the first time really made clear to us how dark it looked for Norway now.

We stood down on the little wharf where the trawler which was to take us was loading medical supplies for Molde. Out over the fjord a black cloud of smoke showed where the town was; we knew that it had been bombed and partly burned; we understood that newspapers were no longer likely to be published there. But still they fought over there. The evening seemed entirely light and quiet, but against the deep-blue sky the shells from the anti-aircraft guns no longer seemed like dots of smoke, they came out like small shining stars. And suddenly there was a star which grew larger and larger, it did not go out, it fell and broke on the way into three falling flames – a plane had been shot down burning. "I beheld Satan as lightning fall from heaven," someone quoted. I had just thought of the same Scripture passage.

It was midnight before we got away. It was black and quiet in the shadow of the high forelands, where we stole along in the shelter of the coast, but the fjord lay pale and shining, and reflected the dark shores and white mountains, and Venus shone large and clear in the pale-green sky.

At the hospital where we landed we again met people who took us in, gave us food, and helped us to get an automobile the next morning. Through fire-ravaged Molde, over mountains where there was still full winter, along new fjord arms, we came out at Bud.

It is the farthest point in Romsdal. Here Norway projects a flat headland of granite rock and heather-grown hills and brown marshes out into the North Sea, which breaks in white waves over the rocks in even the most sunny calm. But the spring had come here too: dwarf willow blossomed so the gold-green dust drifted off it when we walked the paths through the fields of heather. In the quiet inlets between the cliffs eider-ducks sailed, a brown female and a brown and white male, pair by pair; gulls and terns and sea-swallows with their red legs had come home to their old nesting-places. In one of the outports at Hustadviken we went on board one of two trawlers, which were going north. They were full of soldiers and were loaded with ammunition and cannon they had saved when our troops in southern Norway had to surrender. They wanted to get to northern Norway, where the country was still free, and continue in the fight.

The trawler on which we were had berths for six, and there were thirty-six of us. Some German refugees, a well-known author of the extreme Left – he was on his back, palsied and almost paralyzed with rheumatism and sciatica – his young son and daughter, who watched over their sick father as tenderly as two guardian angels, his wife, who volunteered for the job of stewardess. All the others were soldiers.

We sailed at night; during the days we lay hidden in outports between the farthest islands. And day after day the ocean lay quiet and bright, night after night the red of the sunset passed into the red of dawn. And every waking hour and moment I believe we all thought the same thing: that this our country, Norway, is so beautiful; it is past belief that anything so beautiful is real. Stern, wild, with the mountain wall rising straight out of the sea, peaks and crags reaching toward heaven, buried in snow and ice – with few and poor strips of land here and there under the mountain, where there was room for a small farm, or two or three. Nobody has tried to wrest a living from this country except us – and it is ours, ours. We will not give up our right to it, if we must wait a hundred years to get it.

A kind soldier offered me his sleeping bag. Every evening he made it up for me and put me in it. It was hard, but snug and fresh, to lie and sleep out on the deck. In the morning, when I crept out of it, the soldier slipped in and slept some hours. For the man crippled with rheumatism, for whom they had also made a bed on deck, it was surely worse. But there was no word of complaint from him, and his grim humor helped to keep up our spirits on board.

Planes going north frequently passed in along the coast. They took no notice of us, were probably going to Narvik or Bodö. But when we were to pass the outlet of the Trondhjem fjord it became quite exciting. We had heard that the Germans had secured fishing trawlers and were patrolling the seaway here. So we kept far out to sea, and in the early morning we lay in at the harbor of the farthermost lighthouse.

We were lying there when we caught sight of the black trawler – much larger than either of our two – which was cruising outside the entrance of our outport. It disappeared; an hour later it appeared again and headed directly toward us. Cast anchor next to us. The deck was full of young men – they looked at us, silent and suspicious, and we looked at them. They were Norwegians, but were they honest people or some of the Germans' hirelings? It turned out they were soldiers – mostly marines – and they too wanted to get north and fight on. And they had been as afraid of us as we of them.

So we three trawlers sailed together between Nordland's white mountain chain and the islands with the fantastic sculpture-like forms – Lekamöja (the Maiden of Leka), Hestmannen (the Horseman), which resembles a knight with a fluttering mantle, Rödöi (Red Island), shaped like a mighty lion's body.

When we were four hours by sea from Bodö we learned that it was unlikely that civilians would be permitted to land, and if we wanted to go to Tromsö we should have to go beyond the farthest islands in Lofoten, because Vestfjord was full of mines and countermines. But if we wanted to we could go back to Mo in Rana with another trawler. From there it should be possible to go overland to Sweden.

I had little desire to retrace my path. Among other things, I had thought that in Bodö I might perhaps learn something more about the bombing of our hospital ship *Brand IV* outside Aalesund. The head doctor on board, who had been wounded, was the same medical officer with whom Hans had gone. And among the slain was "a young Medical Corps volunteer." But my friends tried to convince me that if it had been my son, his name would have been in the papers. – Later I learned that Hans had left the Medical Corps the second week and had been assigned to messenger service between the army division at Otta and troops which were still behind the German forces; he was a good skier and knew the mountain between Otta and Lillehammer as well as his own pocket. And both Professor Paasche and I had money due us in Sweden – and of course we could not live indefinitely on the hospitality of our countrymen.

The soldiers went on. And the German refugees did not dare to turn back, so they got permission to go farther north on the trawler. God knows what finally became of them.

7

The last stage, from Mo over the border, was the worst.

We started in the afternoon, on a truck. The road went up over the mountain, winding and turning along the steep cliff – it had been driven to pieces, and broken up by melting snow for long stretches. The chauffeur who drove our car performed a real tightrope dance. We jumped to heaven, as we sat and held our seats by clutching one another – we were slung to left and to right, and sometimes the car stuck fast in the thawing holes in the frozen road, and it took an hour's exertion to get it out and under way again. So we did not do more than the first two miles[5] that night. How it was for the man with rheumatism to be shaken and thrown here and there for hours is not easy to imagine.

The same hearty, sympathetic reception at the mountain hut where we stayed the night. It was full of road workers, but they turned out of their bunks for us. The next afternoon about four we continued our journey by foot, with our sick companion on a stretcher which the sons from the mountain home had made and carried.

Midway on the mountain road some automobiles where supposed to be standing, which had not been able to return to Mo. They took us a way – as far as their gas lasted. And finally we had ahead of us a

5 One Norwegian mile is 10 kilometers – approximately 6 English miles.

four-mile ski trip over the mountain to the last farm on the Norwegian side of the border. They had secured a bob-sled for the sick man. When it turned out that I had trouble keeping up with the skiers – it was twenty years since I had last had skis on my feet, and my fur coat was a poor skiing costume – they put me also on the sled. And pulled by six young men we came at long last to the border farm.

Paasche's children had been remarkably brave during the entire trip, but now they could hold out no longer. So the rest of our company stayed there, but the boys who pulled the sled were to go back to their work the next day, so they went on with the sick man and me – and his young son and daughter wanted to be with their father. While the morning light spread over the world of white mountains, we were drawn over the lake which the border crosses, Storuman. The ice was water-sodden, so at times the boys who pulled us sank in up to their knees and the water splashed high up around the sled.

The first golden rays of the morning sun were illuminating the mountain on the Norwegian side when we encountered the first Swedish sentinel. From the Swedish border on, the road was cleared of snow, and while the boys who pulled the sled continued over the fields, the young girl, Dagny, and I took to the country road. She insisted on carrying my bag also – and I did not protest against it as vigorously as I should have.

It was supposed to be about two kilometers to the nearest army post. And when we got there, it turned out there was a full house; we could not stay. It was impossible to use the sled; the sick man had to be carried on his stretcher again. And his daughter and I continued to wade along the country road. Supposedly it was one kilometer – a little more than half a mile – to the next post, and it was said that only a few road workers were staying there. It was daylight now, and in the birch grove all the spring birds of Lapland were raising their voices in full-throated song – but all I wanted was to get into a house and stretch out full length. One kilometer is roughly a thousand strides. I counted and counted; the one kilometer became two and three. And the counting only made me still sleepier. Finally we became afraid we had gone past the place without seeing it, in our half-sleeping state. But at last the little gray hut appeared in a turn of the road. Then it was past five in the morning.

In the hut it was colder than outdoors. A cooking stove in the middle of the floor; along the walls, bunks in which there was a little hay and some withered leaves, all empty but one: in it a man bundled in a red quilt lay and slept like a stone.

At least he was not awakened by our building a fire in the stove; we would at least try to get the room a little warm before the sick man came. So we sat on two backless stools, dozed, and waited. When the bearers came with Dagny's father, the man in the bunk jumped with a start, stared wildly with two sharp blue eyes under tousled yellow hair: "In the name of hell – is it war?" He thought they were carrying in someone who had been wounded.

While we explained the situation, the man put on his trousers and shoes, got the coffee kettle on the fire, and brought out his food supplies. With a free hand he offered the whole company bread and butter, sausage and cheese, coffee and milk. We had been received hospitably at other places, too, but not with such radiantly warm-hearted cordiality, not urged to eat and drink with such a heartfelt merry friendliness as that of this Swedish road worker. His contagiously happy kindness livened us up after fourteen hours of fatigue. Jon Anderson and his pal Jonas, who turned up during the morning, I shall remember with gratitude to the day of my death.

The boys from the mountain hut could not get back to their work that day after all. So we all turned in. It's unbelievable how good it was to lie on the bare wood of the bunk. The last thing of which I was conscious was Jon Anderson, who was hovering about the room with his red quilt – not easy to know whom he should cover with it. Put it under the sick man, we agreed. And the next moment we were all asleep.

Sweden, Summer 1940

 During the day the rest of our party came over the border, accompanied by some soldiers, who said the military authorities would come for us with an automobile and take us down to the customs office and tourist station at Strimasund.

It is far between the farms, and they all look small and poor in Swedish Lapland. The country here is still largely used by the Lapps, who graze their herds of reindeer in the mountains all summer. There is one white knoll behind another, their tops barren, their sides covered with small thickets of birch. All waters here run down to the Ume, the large river along which we were to drive.

Here, too, it was spring, springs as we Nordic people know and love it. The snow still covers everything, but it is melting and fills the air with a fragrant haze all day long; toward evening there is a cold smell of wet stone and of the swelling birch buds. A young laborer who was to go down with us in the car went around showing us all something fine which he guarded tenderly in his large fist: a clump of moss-like green, closely sprinkled with tiny dark rose flowers. He had found it in a sunny mountain crevice, a kind of saxifrage which is the first spring flower up here. He was going to take it down to "his missus," he said proudly. But we were all allowed to hold it a little while and look at it really well.

The motor lorry came, crowded with soldiers. In some way they managed to pack us in. And again it was literally necessary to "hold together"; everyone took hold of the one next to him, and so we jounced down over roads which were almost as terrible as the road on the Norwegian side.

There were swarms of soldiers everywhere. Sweden was fully mobilized. It was the *landstorm* troops – the reservists – who were stationed here, in gray-blue cloaks with dark-blue facings, and three-cornered hats. The uniform is somewhat reminiscent of that worn by Charles XII's soldiers. It was not quite so idiotic as it must have seemed to the eyes of the foreign press when the Russians dressed their handful of Finnish traitors in Teriijoki in old Carolinian uniforms from the museum in Leningrad. The Russians themselves I imagine saw no difference between them and the uniforms which the Swedish infantry used until a few years ago. Now the reservists must wear them out; the infantry have been given gray-green uniforms of the usual European style.

The soldiers began to ask us guarded questions about the war in Norway. And some of them could not resist expressing their dissatisfaction at not having been allowed to help the Norwegians fight. They were silenced by their companions; the reservists are older men, most of them married and the fathers of families. And they were happy so long as they could avoid getting into the war. Among the soldiers whom I met later, in the south of the country, the resentment of Sweden's forced inaction, and the wish to fight were much more common.

The customs inspection at Strimasund was painless, although none of us had passes or, on the whole, anything resembling papers. And at the tourist station the Lottes did all they could to provide us all with beds; it was not easy, for they had the house full of officers. Finally it was arranged, with all the men in one room and the women and children in the other. Still we could not undress – among other reasons because there were alarms here almost every night; it was the time when German planes constantly ranged over Swedish territory. By mistake, it was said; to spy upon Swedish defense preparations, everyone believed. After the Swedes had shot down a number of the planes, things improved. Probably it was chiefly because the Swedes had prepared that they escaped German attack; the losses of men and material in wholly unprepared Norway had been so large, it could hardly have seemed tempting to undertake a Sweden fully armed and ready for battle. Romantic souls – of whom there are more in Sweden than in the other Scandinavian countries – said, moreover, that Hermann Göring was supposed to have promised, on his word of honor as a German officer, that he would never attack his late and beloved

Karin's fatherland. We Norwegians were sure that if Hermann had given such a promise, Sweden could expect to be attacked at the first opportunity.

Next morning at Strimasund Professor Paasche burst in upon us as we stood about in various degrees of undress, washing ourselves: the radio had just brought the news of Hitler's invasion of Holland and Belgium. Some of our party considered this good news: now the war on the western front was beginning in earnest; here the Germans would meet opposition of equal strength; when Hitler could no longer furnish the Germans with victories and conquests at bargain prices, the great peace-loving people would rise against their tyrants. The end of gangster rule, the end of the war – from all the countries which Hitler had forced them to subjugate, the German troops would hurry home to set their own house in order. I was considerably less optimistic; among other things. I have never had a particle of faith in the possibility of Germans' ever giving back anything they have taken, unless it is wrested from them. But the tragedy on the western front was beyond the dreams of my most pessimistic moments.

During the day we were taken farther into Sweden, interned in a little country town, where it was still thicker with soldiers, then taken farther by bus. The officers and soldiers all did what they could to be helpful and pleasant. Only an occasional small local official could not hide his nervousness because his district was being overrun by such dangerous people as Norwegian refugees must be, and gave vent to his irritation at the situation. The bus we were sent south in was so full it seemed impossible that room could be made for more passengers. A company of Finnish children and old women who had been refugees in northern Norway was now fleeing back to Finland. "The Finns can ride for nothing, the Norwegians must pay," the chauffeur decreed.

At each stop people were waiting to take the bus. Dagny and I were ordered to give up our places to two telephone workers: "Then one of them will take the old woman" – that was me – "and the other the young girl on his knee." All four of us obeyed with solemn faces, though the one who was allotted "the young girl" looked as if he would have liked to smile. A little later both workmen dug around in their pockets and brought out a Swedish five-kroner bill apiece that they wanted to give us: "For coffee and a little food on the way." We thanked them, rather moved, but explained that it wasn't so bad for us; when we reached Storuman we could get money from friends in Sweden; there were surely many refugees who needed it still more than we. The men nodded. At the station where they got off I saw then one of them, at least, gave his bill to a woman from Mo in Rana, who was going to try to reach a sister farther north in Lapland.

It seemed quite unreal to come into an actual hotel again – a Swedish tourist hotel, arranged with Swedish taste and comfort, excellently managed, as almost all Swedish hotels are. Only the warm water to which we had looked forward did not materialize; there was fuel-rationing and the warm-water apparatus was shut off. But the maids at the hotel carried up hot water in buckets, with angelic kindness. And the young hairdresser in the little station town was willing to come and give Stina Paasche and me shampoos, although it was the second day of Pentecost, and a holiday in Sweden.

The two or three small shops in the town were almost stripped of goods, there had been so many refugees who had come as we did, with little more than the clothes on their backs. I needed some handkerchiefs, but the only ones they had left were the black-bordered kind which Swedish peasants carry at funerals. I do not usually pay attention to "warnings," but now I was anxious about Hans, and I did not like it. That was why Stina and I laughed and jested a good deal about my fine new funeral handkerchiefs.

2

From time to time we had said good-by to most of our traveling companions. Our friend with the lumbago had to stay on at the hotel to rest for some days, in a good bed. At a station midway between Storuman and Stockholm the Paasches and I parted; Mrs. Paasche is Swedish and they were to stay awhile with her relatives there. It was a light spring night – the sky as clear as glass and pale green along the horizon, the kind of night we Norwegians love, although they make us melancholy and half-sick with longing for the summer, which now is near, which always leaves us again before before we have half-quenched our thirst for warmth and sunshine and green fields. And now we had the whole of Norway to long for; we thought we were so homesick already that we could not bear it.

My friend Alice had telegraphed to me at Storuman, inviting me to stay with her. Her son had been mobilized, so I could have his room, and my married sister in Stockholm had no guest room.

They both met me at the station. They were moved, but not more than was natural, I thought, after all that had happened. Not until the next day did Alice tell me that Anders had fallen in the fighting at Segelstad bridge as early as the 27th of April. She had wanted to let me rest a day first before she told it. Hans, they believed, had come home to Lillehammer after the surrender; at any rate it was certain that he had not been on board the *Brand IV* when the hospital ship was bombed by the Germans.

3

My impressions from Sweden in the summer of 1940 are one-sided: all my Swedish friends had the same attitude toward the Nazis as I.

It is true, there were circles in Sweden that were very friendly to the Nazis. During the former World War most of the Swedish upper class – the nobility, the officers, the financiers, the leaders of Swedish industry and trade – were pronouncedly pro-German. And the broad middle class, which at that time at any rate preferred to be of the same opinion as the nobility and the army, was even more strongly German in its sympathies. The "Storsvenske" faction (as we nicknamed the Swedish nationalists) seems to have dreamed a foggy dream that a great and victorious Germany would make the "Germanic" nations lords of Europe, or the world, and under the leadership of Germany Sweden in some way or other would also regain something of its position as a great power which it had, before Charles XII ruined the country with his warlike exploits and lost it the control of the Baltic Sea. Opposed to the "Storsenske" party stood everything in Sweden which represented freedom of thought, liberal and radical political thinking. These circles had shown themselves true friends of Norway in 1905 when we broke away from the union with Sweden. There is no reason to doubt that Oscar II, who was then the King of Sweden and Norway, would never have gone to war against a people who had been his subjects. He regarded his relation to his subjects as paternal, and although he was Swedish, body and soul, he certainly loved Norway – as a feudal lord loves his younger son, a bothersome child and less important from a family point of view, but nevertheless his child. But it is uncertain whether the conflict between Norway and Sweden could have been settled peacefully if the Swedish Left party and the Social Democrats and a great many of the Swedish artists and intellectuals had not been so definitely opposed to war and the use of force against Norway, the most democratic country in Scandinavia, Ibsen's and Björnstjerne Björnson's country. It is equally certain that if Norway and Sweden had still been united in 1914 in a personal union under a Bernadotte king, with Sweden as the leading country in the union, the "brother peoples" could hardly have avoided getting into the war – on the side of Germany. All my Swedish friends belonged to this circle of liberals. Politically most of them were Social Democrats. Many had been Communists, up to the time when the attack on Finland opened their eyes to the fact that Stalin Communism is only a new and more brutal edition of Czarist Russia's worst tendencies – the desire to add to its power by conquering its neighbors' territory and by keeping the masses in a kind of half-slavery, the indifference to the life and welfare of the individual, which will always be incomprehensible to people of a Christian and democratic society, however imperfectly they practice their Christianity and their democracy. It is characteristic of Norwegian and Swedish idealism that from the very circle of young people who had "believed in Russia" numbers flocked to Finland, to serve as soldiers or civil workers in the war against

Stalin, the new Herod who had murdered their savior of the world in his cradle. Though it is unjust to say, as was often said, that Stalin's war was primarily a war against the homes of the Finnish workers, that ambulances, churches, and buildings marked with the Red Cross were the objectives which the Soviet bombers preferably sought, the men in the Mannerheim Line were bombed severely enough, and hundreds of thousands of Russian soldiers were slaughtered like cattle before the wall of Finland's defenders. But in the summer of 1940 the disillusioned Swedish Communists were still wild with pain and hatred against a Soviet Russia which had robbed them of their hope of eternal bliss which was to become a reality in the Russian workers' and peasants' republic.

The entire circle of my acquaintances in Sweden were then anti-Nazis. But it is certain that the Germans already had succeeded in reducing the numbers of their friends and adherents quite appreciably. There were several thousand Germans in Stockholm, and nobody doubted that they had their instructions from the present German regime – every single man or woman who had come into the country in the last seven or eight years, exactly as had proved true in Norway. And Sweden, which was almost completely encircled between the hereditary enemy, Russia, and its former friend, Germany, was in a difficult position, forced to give consideration to the desires of the dictator states, often to a degree which must seem almost intolerable to a nation which, generation after generation, has cherished its "glorious memories" from the time when Swedish hero kings and Swedish soldiers cast their swords in the balance whenever the fate of Europe was being decided.

The Germans' unfailing ability to destroy whatever sympathy they may have won, wherever anyone has any sympathy with them – an ability which is even more eminent than their ability to organize their human and material resources – became evident here also. The Prussian King who ran after his terror-stricken subjects on the streets, his pigtail flying, his cane raised on high, crying frantically: *"Ihr sollt mich lieben! Ihr sollt mich lieben!"* ("You shall love me! You shall love me!") – that is the eternal German.

I do not deny that I was entertained when a couple of relatives of Göring's first wife whom I met expressed their bitter disappointment in Nazism. One, a lady, was deeply grieved, she had been so fond of Hermann, and her beloved Karin had given her life for this movement which had turned out so sadly. Another, a young doctor, with a name belonging to the old Swedish nobility, explained that some years ago he had been with Göring for fourteen days, at one of the family's manorhouses. He had heard that fellow rant hour after hour every single day. Since then his hatred and scorn of Nazism had been boundless. He had recently had difficulty with the authorities because of the violent language in some of his articles about the new Germany.

4

Yngve, Alice's husband, busied himself getting me the necessary papers, including ration cards. When I came to Stockholm only a very few articles, imports, were rationed. Except soap, even though Sweden normally manufactures enough soap for its own and for export. And the warm-water apparatus where we lived was shut off. We heated water in the kitchen for a warm bath now and then; otherwise we had to manage with cold showers.

Blackouts did not play such a large role in Stockholm; in the middle of May it is light until late evening. All the same, we were happy when after a time they were abolished; it was pleasant to be able to light the lamps without first having to set up the dark screens before the windows. And then Stockholm has relatively more open-air restaurants than any other city in Europe, with the possible exception of Copenhagen. And nowhere in the world are they so delightful as in Stockholm: many of them were once old roadside taverns celebrated by the poet Bellman, with a fragrance of the love of life and beauty characteristic of the time of Gustavus III over the simple interiors, and with a splendor of flowers which I have never seen equaled elsewhere. But in the evening it is most beautiful of all, when the lanterns are lighted between the huge old trees and illuminate the vault of young green leaves. We went out a good deal in the evenings to sit and look at it; there was a kind of farewell mood everywhere. No Swedes cherished any illusions about the future. At best, Sweden would probably escape being drawn into the war, but the encirclement, the loss of all the country's markets except Germany (which itself decided what and with what it would pay), the vast expenditures for defense, the mobilizing which kept the young men away from their occupations and studies, together meant the end of that "prosperity" which Sweden had utilized so wisely and well. It was not likely that next summer anyone could afford to be so prodigal with flowers as we had got used to being in the Scandinavian countries. We are always hungry for sun and summer. And as soon as we had raised our standard of living we tried to make summer a continuous flower festival. There was an overwhelming profusion of flowers, of colors and fragrances – in the parks around the noble old buildings in the middle of the city, in the parks surrounding the new workers' homes, around farmhouses and poor cottages, in the flower shops and in the marketplaces, on the verandas and in everyone's front windows.

But the Swedes were far from certain of peace. Compared with other capitals throughout the world Stockholm was still a pattern of civic order and cleanliness. But we who had known the city before noticed façades which had not received their annual cleaning, frame houses which needed painting, streets damaged by frost which had not been repaired so carefully as usual. People said it openly – there was no sense in it if the Russians or Germans were to bomb us some fine day.

The Swedes walked around and looked at their capital. The sunshine glittered white on the water of the lake, Mälar, and the stream from the Baltic Sea which meet under the bridges in the center of the city; the air shimmered with a light silvery fog. In the most ancient part of town, on the castle island, the interiors of the old stone houses from the Middle Ages had to a great extent been rebuilt, made modern and practical, but the decorative gabled façades had been allowed to remain untouched. Here and there, to provide air and light for the narrow, crooked streets, a block of buildings without great artistic value had been torn down and a beautiful little open square created. In the outskirts of the city were situated large blocks of new hospitals and old people's homes, new scientific centers, entirely new sections of the city with particularly beautiful, modern homes for people of all income groups. The picturesque old slum quarters, with small yellow and green and red wooden buildings, had been made sanitary where it was possible; where it was not possible they had been replaced by something new which was also beautiful. I did not meet one Swede who did not want Sweden to defend itself to the utmost if the country were attacked, even if all Stockholm and all the other beloved and beautiful cities should be reduced to ruins. But that they hoped it could be avoided was very natural.

Every time I came down on the elevator, the first thing I saw was the placard which had been placed opposite it in the hall, informing us that there were bomb-proof rooms in the cellar under the building. In all the streets there were signs at short intervals showing the way to the nearest shelters. And they were working to make ready more and larger shelters in the rocky ground under the market-places and parks; all day long we heard the boom of the blasting. Strangely enough, it was harder on my nerves than the explosion of the bombs that hit and the crack of anti-aircraft guns had been at home in Norway. And the whistling of the steamships in the harbor and the drone of the Swedish planes which cruised over the city at night woke me again and again; at home I had often gone to sleep in spite of alerts and the enemy planes which were passing over the house.

Alice was busy with a historical work, so she had frequent errands at the public libraries. I went with her; I wanted to note down some of the opinions expressed by Danish writers from the Middle Ages about their neighbors, the Germans – Saxons they were called then. In the reading-rooms, at the circulation desks, one saw almost no one but young girls, women students, some old men, and what the Swedes call *"kronvrak"* (crown wreckage), conscripts who have been rejected as physically unfit.

The young girls and the boys under the age of compulsory military service – among others, my nephew, who had just entered the University – had registered for volunteer work in the country. The farmers were suffering from the shortage of labor. And the drought began to be dangerous when it continued into June. There had not been a good rain since the previous fall, and little snow had fallen in the winter, which had been one of the coldest in the memory of man. A Finnish friend of mine, who had lost all he possessed – his beautiful old ancestral estate was situated near Viborg, and now was probably falling into ruin as a result of Russian disorder and filth – said that the apple trees all over Finland had frozen to death during the winter of the war, among them the couple of thousand which he had planted on his former property; and although he felt toward the Russians as did all other Finns, he could not help grieving over the dead trees. He had lost his wife the year before the war broke out. At that time her death had almost crushed him. Now he was happy, she had escaped experiencing the bitter peace.

5

I thought the same thing each morning when I took in the paper and glanced through the latest war news, as I went to go to mass at the small

Dominican chapel on Linné Street: "Thank God that Anders does not have to experience this." Who among us dared to hope that England would be able to defend her life for many weeks if France also was overrun? Least of all we Norwegians, with our dearly bought experience of how wretchedly unprepared England had shown herself in Norway, how uselessly the untrained young English boys had been slaughtered in our mountain passes.

Anders had lived in England four years, as a "prentice" at Austin's factories and a student at Birmingham Technical University. For him, as for me, England was the dearest place in the world next to Norway. In the foundries, in the forges, in all the departments of the large factory, his companions had been English workers, and he could never praise them enough for their tact, their kindly and good-hearted reserve. They even had a certain kindness toward Nazi Germany: "Perhaps we were too hard on them when they had lost the war; one should not hit a man when he is down." They were embarrassed and blushed when the newspapers and radio told of completely hysterical outbreaks of German Hitler-worship. That sexual perversion had ravaged some groups of people in England also, the workers were quite aware, and their healthy instinct told them that the Hitler enthusiasm was in part an outcropping of this same sickness, to which the trenches of the previous World War had given an impetus. The factory workers in Northfield grew red and mumbled: "I say, but they must be crazy, you know;

I think we ought to have done something to help them before they got as cracked as all that."

In northern Norway a Norwegian army and fleet still fought shoulder to shoulder with Englishmen, Poles, and French *chasseurs alpins* – these last and the people up there were as congenial as Scotch and soda. But bad news continued to stream in: Holland was defeated, Belgium had been forced to surrender, France – no, we could not give up the hope that a miracle would happen. *"O God, sauvez, sauvez la France, au Nom du Sacré Coeur,"* we sang in the Dominicans' church, in the mass for the souls of fallen Norwegians and French soldiers in Norway.

Meanwhile I had learned certainly that Hans had come home to Lillehammer, well and unwounded, after the capitulation in southern Norway. Now he was in Oslo, but would try to get the necessary papers so he could join me in Sweden. I had received telegrams from friends in America, offers to write magazine articles, requests to carry through the lecture tour for which I had signed contracts early in the winter, when the plan had been that I should talk among other things about Finland's fight. But I could do nothing before I had got my son out of the German-occupied country; we had heard enough of their use of hostages.

While we waited for news about Hans, Yngve and Alice proposed that we should visit Hammarby, Linné's estate on the plain outside Uppsala. Among the works which I had planned and started before I left Norway was a popular biography of Carl von

Linné – such a work is lacking in Norwegian. And ever since my earliest youth Linné has been for me a kind of secular patron saint. The wonderful fragrance of youth and joy of discovery in his books about his travels in Sweden, the charm of his autobiographical notes, the intense and sensitive nature which reveals itself in a thousand surprising ways in whatever he has written, had always captivated me. And the stern and manly faith in the notes about *Nemesis Divina* which he wrote for his son after he himself was a death-doomed man, that had taken on a new significance for me in these days. The minister's son from the poor country home was born just as Sweden's days as a great power were drawing to a close – Charles XII was leading Swedish armies here and there on the continent, far from their fatherland; at home in Sweden women and children and old people toiled to keep the people alive during the years of want. Carl Linnaeus gave his country a new position as a great power, in the international world of natural science which was just coming into being. He himself had attained material success to a greater degree than most people – that he was elevated to the nobility was at this time nothing unusual: at least half of the families who are inscribed in the Swedish or Finnish *Riddarhuset* (House of the Nobility) are descended from men who were ennobled for their services to their country, as soldiers, scholars, administrators, artists. Prosperity made him neither optimistic nor pessimistic; Baron von Linné knew what he had always known: God rules the world with a hard, righteous hand; sooner or later His vengeance overtakes each and every one who has practiced deceit and unrighteousness; "The conquered have a weapon still, they appeal to God."

We went out to Hammarby one morning late in May. It clouded over while we drove across the large open Upland plain, with its pale-green fields and ashen-gray plow land; it looked as if we should at last get the longed-for rain. We were the only visitors at Hammarby that day. Linné's mansion is not large: a central building and two wings are only two-story red-painted frame houses. Many farms in my part of Norway have grander buildings. The garden outside is somewhat as it must have been in Linné's time, planted according to his own notes. But "Russia," that part of the garden where he had set out the plants sent him by Catherine the Great from her kingdom, had become once more a copse of Swedish foliage trees. Only a light-yellow kind of larkspur from Siberia had made itself at home here; it grew like a weed over the whole property.

We walked through the deserted rooms. They are marked by an almost Spartan simplicity, but the plain painted wooden furniture is evidence that Swedish taste has always been sure and distinguished. Linné's bedroom and workroom are papered with the pages from a great work about exotic plants – he cut it up and pasted the engravings on the walls so he could look at them while he thought out his works. Alice told a provocative story about an old Swedish authoress who after a dinner for Ibsen had kissed the tablecloth where the master's hand had rested. I laughed, but then I did it all the same – kissed the top of the writing-desk, where Linné's hand must so often have rested.

Later we sat out under the trees, where the wife of the caretaker serves coffee and bread and butter. It began to rain, a fine, close rain, and we drank in the good smell of wet earth and new grass. And Alice whispered the quotation I had sat and thought of all the time:

"The conquered have a weapon still, they appeal to God."

6

Norway was not yet conquered. In northern Norway we fought, not without success, against the Germans. That part of our army which was stationed there had been mobilized after the Finnish war broke out. They had opportunity to show that our boys had in them the making of soldiers as good as the Finns. It is a bitter thought – what we could have accomplished against the invasion army in southern Norway if our boys had had sufficient training and war material.

As it was, they had accomplished *something*. One day I had a visit from a soldier who had fought in Anders's troop, had been one of those who had brought his body in from the woods during the night; his companions carried it with them when they had to give up the position at the bridge. Anders had had command of three machine-guns, they had been in action from the time when the battles had been fought north of Oslo, at Bleiken, Saeter, at Hadeland, home again to Gudbrandsdal. The worst of it had been that time after time they had to give up positions on the mountainside which commanded a piece of road and which they could have held for weeks – that is, if a bomb did not just happen to smash them – if we had only had enough men to hold the side roads, which lead from one valley over into the next, and enough weapons and enough ammunition. But always they had to retreat because the Germans were at their backs. But they had done pretty well. "At one place we counted almost two hundred German soldiers lying in heaps along the country road, dead and wounded. That must be a great comfort to you?" It is.

And Anders had shown himself such a splendid officer, quiet, brave, resourceful in making the best possible use of the few men and what little they had of equipment. "And then, you know, he was such an incomparably kind person." *Snill* – the untranslatable Norwegian word; *kind* comes nearest to it, but *snilhet* must be quiet in manner, undemonstrative; kindness does not always have to be that. But for most Norwegians the best that can be said of a person is that he is *snill*.

The soldier was an older Norwegian, living in

Sweden and a Swedish citizen. He had happened to be in Lillehammer on April 10. When a motor lorry full of soldiers who were going to Jörstadmoen whizzed past him on the street, he signaled them and managed to fling himself on it. Afterward he had been with them during the whole campaign. But for him, of course, the war was ended now, "for the present, at any rate," he laughed quietly. "If the day comes when we can think of driving out that gang, then I must hope to do my share."

But almost every day soldiers came to me who imagined that I could help them so they could get back to Norway by way of Lapland and get into the war again. There was not much I could do; it was on the whole not easy for the boys who had come into Sweden to make the journey back to the front in Norway. But some of them managed it.

Finally, one of the last days in May, I received a telegram from Hans – he had been interned in a military post on the Swedish side of the border, but expected to be able to leave one of the first days. Seldom have I been happier than that morning I met him at the station in Stockholm.

He had obtained a passport in Oslo and had been promised that the German authorities would grant him a permit to leave. But then the Germans demanded that he come up to their office once more, they wanted to talk to him. On that occasion he learned that the chief of the Gestapo in Oslo was a former *Wienergutt* and talked perfect Norwegian. He had the impression that they could demand promises from him that he could not give. So he dressed as if he were going for a walk in town – the Germans were suspicious of sport clothes – took a train to an out-of-the-way station in one of the forest provinces near the Swedish border, boarded one of the buses there, and rode until he passed a path in the woods which looked promising. In the woods he met several young Norwegians; they were quite a little party when they came to the first Swedish military post, after a trip of four Norwegian miles through the woods.

The Germans had guards at all the roads leading from Norway into Sweden, but it was impossible for them to watch a boundary which runs for miles through pathless woods. They were afraid to go about in our woods. Small patrolling parties who ventured there had small prospects of getting out again alive. It did not help that the Germans took "ruthless" revenge wherever they had been shot at by civilians, or thought they had. On a quite small farm up in Gudbrandsdal, where Hans and I knew the family, the Germans took the only "man" who was at home, a boy of eleven, and shot him against the barn door, while his mother and little sister had to watch, because they claimed German soldiers had been shot at from this farm. At that time there were still Norwegian soldiers in the forest at both sides. But the Germans' fear of snipers was completely hysterical – and incomprehensible to the Norwegians, who had seen them advance, densely massed and under command, with absolute contempt of death; why should it be so horrible to be shot at by civilians with hunting guns and rifles? On the farms up through the valley, where German soldiers stayed overnight, they did not dare "go out" after nightfall (instead of toilets most Norwegian farms have well-kept comfortable little houses beside the stables). So several of the farmers whose houses had been burned to the ground consoled themselves that it would have been impossible anyhow to have got their houses so clean as to rid them of the smell of *Deutschtum*. In Norway people had already got the impression that singly or in small groups which are not certain of superiority in numbers and materials the majority of Germans are far from courageous, – at any rate as we Norwegians understand courage. And naturally Norwegian farmers – and farmers' wives – could not comprehend that it was any crime to protect their homes against strangers who try to break in. We were not used to war and we are used to showing hospitality toward all who come to our homes and behave well, but if anyone tries to force his way in, we throw him out, quite unceremoniously.

Hans naturally had a good deal to tell of what he had seen of the war in Norway – of the Germans' use of civilians, women and children also, whom they would drive before them as they advanced, to keep the Norwegian soldiers from attacking. In some places it had been successful, in others not; the civilians themselves had in many places called out to our boys: "Shoot, shoot, never mind us." He named a couple of our acquaintances in the valley who had been killed or wounded in this way. Hove agricultural school, outside Lillehammer, had been shot to bits, although the roofs of all the buildings were marked with great red crosses. On the whole, people in Norway had not found that red crosses were any protection against the Germans – quite the opposite. The explanation may be, according to what Hans knew from personal observation, that German soldiers from the Medical Corps had marched or bicycled in the midst of the infantry or artillery, as heavily armed as anyone else. So they presumably expected that we also would misuse the Red Cross.

Hans had bicycled down to Kapp, on the other side of Lake Mjösen, to tell his brother's fiancée that Anders had fallen. Along the road there was almost complete destruction; for a quarter of an hour at a time he had not passed a single dwelling which had not been burned down. At several places the Germans had crammed a building full of their own fallen and set fire to it – it is the same story which Lars Moën tells from Belgium: they tried to conceal how great their losses had been. In that way they burned down among other places the old church in Kvam – one of our most beautiful wooden churches. The common German soldiers, however, were not sure all the fallen were dead before they were burned. Atrocity stories circulated among them, that the ruling Nazis had decided that after this war the sight of war cripples would not spoil the nation's joy in victory. Transport planes which carried the severely wounded back to Germany were supposed to be equipped with a trapdoor, and when the plane was well out in the Skagerrak the wounded were dropped into the sea. This story is probably not true, although the same rumor, or something similar, has been told from other occupied countries. But it is certain that many German soldiers told it and believed it.

Partly, perhaps, it derived from the fact that the Germans' treatment of their wounded was unsatisfactory. Norwegian doctors were horrified at their German colleagues. A few older men, who had received their training before Hitler's time, were of course fully competent. But the younger party doctors knew, as a Norwegian chief doctor expressed it, "less than any wise woman in the Norwegian countryside." The Germans had also sent up some hundred *braune Schwestern,* Nazi nurses. They were strong, hard-working women, but their concepts of cleanliness were not up to date – they were of all degrees, from the "not very clean" to those that in good Norwegian we call "dirty sows." Several of them expressed to Norwegians with whom they had associations that they were enchanted with the beautiful country "which Hitler had presented them."

The abominable bellowing of the Germans when they attacked – which made the Norwegian soldiers consider them repulsive vermin rather than people – was caused to some degree, according to what

Norwegian doctors said, by the fact that before they were sent into action they were given some small chocolate squares which contained cocaine. Quite a small dose, according to the analysis given on the wrapper – Hans had seen some of these wrappers – but the Norwegians had also found some of the chocolate squares, and one of our doctors who examined them said that in reality the amount of cocaine was three times as large as was stated on the wrapper. They had made a couple of Norwegian boys who had eaten a square, "just for fun," dreadfully sick. So we think they must have been accustomed to using cocaine in this way over a longer period.

For that matter, the forces which the Germans had brought into Norway were at least in part such sad human specimens that the Norwegians were much amazed. The young officers were clearly the product of careful physical culture. The ordinary soldiers were armed like traveling fortresses – down to boot-legs stuffed with hand-grenades. But among the men themselves there were an unbelievable number of bowlegged, narrow-shouldered, flat-footed individuals, with broad, drooping bottoms. To the Norwegians it naturally seemed very remarkable that so many wore glasses; in Norway it is relatively uncommon to see people under forty-five with spectacles. Probably no particularly magnificent physique is needed for sitting on tanks and armored cars or operating machines for mass slaughter. All the same, people in Norway were surprised – not least when the Germans took their ease wherever they had made themselves victors; when they rested they undressed, lay and took sun baths along roads and streets. As Hans said: "We are not prudish, you know. But to make a public display of such ugly carcasses we think is indecent.

7

Narvik was recaptured by Norwegian and Allied troops on May 29. The Germans retreated along the railroad line toward Sweden, sharply pursued. It was the first defeat Germany had suffered in this war, Narvik the first loot which had been wrested from Germany's mailed fist. It had squeezed the little town to bits, but never mind – we had taken back the first small piece of the country which is ours.

Then came the news that the Allies were withdrawing their troops from Norway. And on June 8 Norway had to give up, after sixty days of war. At that time no other of the invaded countries had fought so long.

Well, we knew that in all circumstances the fate of our country would be decided at that theater of war where the ultimate battle would be fought. They were black days, but we did not give up hope.

Bad news, however, came thick and fast: the devastation in northern France, the wretched state of the refugees along the roads where we had traveled, young and happy, the French lines breaking here and there, the threat against Paris, which we all regarded as a kind of spiritual capital. Although I was fonder of England, and felt at home there in quite another way than in France, still France was the motherland of ideas of good and evil which had always been fruitful in Scandinavian intellectual life and Scandinavian art.

We thought a miracle must happen. In the hour of utmost need a reserve of unsuspected strength would break out of the soil of France; something must happen so France would not be conquered. It happened in England, where surely not many had expected it would happen.

There was, then, no northern Norway to which Hans and I could go. So it had to be America for us. I hurried to get the necessary visas, photographs, doctors' certificates and all the other papers we had to have. At first I had arranged to travel by way of Petsamo. Then it was said at the Finnish consulate that all space on the boats had been taken until late fall. And who could know how long the steamship connection between Petsazmo and America could be kept open? It must be the long way through Russia and Siberia, via Japan and the Pacific Ocean. I had to have more papers, more visas, more pictures, more certificates.

Yngve hurried around with me; he had bother enough for my sake. Alice made a list of things she thought would be useful on my trip through Russia. And her gifts, pillow and pillow-case, soap – from her rationed supply – came to good use. Two rolls of toilet paper turned out to be the most valuable of all.

Hans and I made reservations in the plane which was to go from Stockholm to Moscow on July 13. Through Intourist we secured tickets all the way to Kobe; through a Swedish tourist bureau we ordered reservations on the *President Cleveland* from Kobe to San Francisco. The period of waiting in Japan they could tell us only approximately. "But about that you may be happy," consoled Yngve. He brought me a book with descriptions of Japan's beauties and attractions. "And clothes are so cheap there – wait to buy for Hans and yourself until you get to Japan." Hans had come over the border with all his baggage in a briefcase, so our wardrobe was of the scantiest.

Some days before we were to leave, Alice gave a party for me. She had invited especially friends who knew America – a Swedish scientist and his wife who had just returned after several years there, a young painter with his sweet American wife. The American Minister, Mrs. Borden Harriman, accepted Alice's invitation, for which we were all happy and thankful. Her helpfulness and kindness toward all Norwegians in Stockholm was magnificent. I had benefited by it myself in many ways. And Alice, like most Swedish ladies, is a master at arranging beautiful parties. – It turned out to be one of the saddest parties at which I have been present. We understood something was brewing, and many of the guests had firsthand acquaintance with what it was, and were bitterly disheartened at what they had learned. Still we had a pleasant time in a way – as one can in spite of everything enjoy oneself at a funeral, because one is with people one prizes. But it seemed a kind of funeral.

The next day it was in all the newspapers. Sweden had felt it necessary to grant the Germans the right to send troops through Sweden to Norway. The Germans had promised they would be only soldiers going to Germany on leave. But now there were not many people in Sweden either who placed any faith in what Germans "promise."

Early in the morning of July 13 we said good-by to my sister, Alice, and Yngve at the square of Nybroplan, where the bus starts which takes passengers to the airport at Bromma.

Fourteen Days in Russia

 The plane that was going to Moscow that day proved to be Russian. I confess I was a little uneasy when I discovered it. Friends who had taken part in the Finnish war could tell harrowing stories of the Russians' dealing with modern machinery of every kind; as a rule they knew nothing about how to handle it and were too careless to be disturbed by the fact that they knew nothing. So I consoled myself – in the war the Russians had relied on numbers; they had people enough to sacrifice. On an important plane route they would certainly employ the type my Norwegian Communist friends were so much taken with – young people, eager to learn, religiously enthusiastic about all the wonders of the machine world. I set my mind at rest and enjoyed the sight of the Swedish skerries from the air.

Tallinn – Rita – lay glittering below us with towers and spires and the river which divides into many arms through the city. We landed on a field where great numbers of planes were standing. The lunch counter in the airport was crowded with Latvian officers and soldiers, many with their heads bandaged or with their arms in slings. We knew that the future looked threatening for Latvia, but we hoped that perhaps it would go better than it looked.

We had not yet broken ourselves of the old optimistic way of thinking that some miracle or other would occur so a small country which was not strong enough to defend itself by force of arms could escape the fate intended for it by the totalitarian states. – The station in Tallinn was attractive and modern, there was a good lunch counter, a "Ladies Room" – not different from other places in Europe. And people were dressed and groomed like the people we were used to seeing. – A few weeks later Latvia's saga was ended – for the present. Murder and want, blood and filth and mismanagement and stench and lice must have engulfed it now.

Through a fairy world of mighty summer clouds of billowing white, sun-gilded, dark blue below, we flew and tried to catch a glimpse of the fabulous Soviet realm between, each time we headed into a new bank of clouds. The country seemed a rolling plain, laced through with threads of shining water. The forest carpets were flecked with the poisonous green of swamps, the desolate and bottomless Russian swamps of which we were to see so much along the way. On higher ground at long intervals a village of tiny light-gray houses, scattered along a pale track of road which looked as if it had made itself, a virgin pure and innocent of anything which could be called engineers. It seemed beautiful, but rather dreary, seen from the air.

We landed at Velikie Luki, the first airport in Russia. I at least thought it was quite exciting to set foot on the soil of the Soviet realm. Was it not a new world to enter? And Velikie Luki did not look at all bad. A paved road between hedges of thriving dogwood led from the landing-place up to the customs station. In front of it a touchingly primitive little garden was laid out, and the room we entered was no dirtier than I had seen elsewhere, in southern Europe, for instance. And it was full of flowers – large potted plants, and bouquets of wild flowers thrust artlessly into empty bottles and old salt jars. There was a restaurant also, not so dirty that we did not dare to order tea in a glass and some strange cakes that tasted of nothing. After I had seen more of Russian management I got the idea that it must be because the Swedish plane personnel passes regularly through Velikie Luki that it was so different from everything else I saw in Russia.

I got some money changed into Russian coins and watched with interest the play of the man's fingers on the abacus. I knew that before they became playthings for babies they had also served in Europe as an aid to figuring, but it was strange to see them in use. Examination of the baggage took hours, but I had secured a letter from the Russian Minister in Stockholm. It worked like a charm, I escaped opening our few small trunks. Afterward I sat on a bench in the sun and enjoyed the view over a boundless plain with some dilapidated old frame houses and, between half-dead poplars, an old unused white church. But eventually the signal was given for us to get into the plane again.

According to the time-table we were now to fly direct to Moscow. But five or six young girls and boys had come on board. They had no baggage; they were bareheaded and without wraps, the girls in flimsy summer dresses and slippers. So in my naïveté I thought we were to make a stop on the way, and young Russia was perhaps taking the plane as we take a bus. And to tell the truth, although it is the intermediate landings that make me dislike flying – they always hurt my ears – I longed heartily to be rid of these young people. I have never been able to learn the correct names of the various rooms and parts of a plane – I am, to repeat, not air-minded – but the Russians went in and out of the compartment where the pilot sat, left the door open, lighted and threw burning cigarette stubs and matches over the entire floor – where a stream of something oily and black which had been oozing out ever since we were over the Baltic Sea grew wider and wider. I speculated intensely on what the black fluid could be – if it were something inflammable.

And then I understood, from the clock, and from seeing that the buildings on the plain below were crowding into clumps of new factories and residence sections, that we must be over Moscow.

The friends who met us drove by an indirect route so we could see a little of the city, before we came to the hotel. And it was certainly true, we got the feeling that we had dropped from the skies into another world.

We were told that before the former World War

Moscow had two million inhabitants. Now it has four million. And there has been no appreciable increase in housing accommodations in the interim. In the factories three shifts work for eight-hour periods, but a great many people also live and sleep in one room in three shifts. I received the impression that two of Moscow's millions walk about the streets day and night. I have never seen such an endless moving stream of people. There are perhaps almost as many people on Broadway in the evening, or in New York's business section when traffic is at its height. But in Moscow the crowds of people walked and walked and walked at all times of the day and night at which I saw anything of the city; during the four days I was there I got a strange feeling that my sense of time was disintegrating. And nothing which could give a hint of why they were walking there – not a shop was open. (On Sunday morning we discovered in a remote quarter of the city an endless queue of people before a tiny dry-goods shop – the kind of which there are some at Lillehammer, where old maids deal in calicoes and sewing materials and the town news, without expecting much profit from the business.) It was said that this shop in Moscow had been sent some rolls of cotton goods from the factory. So it was kept open until the supply was sold out – in a couple of hours. After that those in the queue who had not obtained any had to go home again, and the shop sank back into its Sleeping Beauty lethargy; the state-appointed employees got a holiday, for an indefinite time. On Monday I found a bookshop, connected with the University, which was open – but more of that later. The dust lay thick on the few faded articles which served as window displays. Chiefly they were papier-mâché imitations of hams and cakes. But at one place I saw some baby hats which the sun had faded to a uniform gray-brown and some children's clumsy shoes of felt in a window. One could not imagine that these shops had ever been opened or ever would be opened again.

Our friends took us for a drive around the walls of the Kremlin. Seen from one of the bridges over the river, it looked magnificent in a way, on the river bank, with the evening sun on the strange old watch-towers in the wall and the gilded bulbous domes on the old churches inside the wall. But I must admit I thought the whole was more strange and alien than beautiful. Frankly, I do not believe I should have been enthusiastic about Czarist Moscow either. The Vassilij Cathedral on the Red Square, covered with glazed tiles in strange, brilliant colors, from the foundation to the top of the bulbous domes, looked Oriental – without the finesse, the refinement of taste, of the Oriental buildings in Asia Major – that is, to judge by pictures. All the monumental old buildings from the 1820's – the University of Moscow, for example – resembled buildings of the same period in Europe (and America), but they were heavier, clumsier, with their unfunctional open stairways and colonnades and façades. It is true that Moscow is a mixture of the East and the West. But in whatever style Russian architects choose to express themselves – Oriental or modern classic, the style of Baron Hausmann's Paris in some of the administration buildings in the Red Square, the style of Russia's rural frame buildings, with the broad carved window-frames carried over into molded brick, the most modern style experiments of the West copied in the Soviet period's immense new buildings – the Russian versions are always more clumsy, less beautiful, or more positively ugly than their prototypes. But I must confess I may be so constituted by nature that nothing Russian can awaken a sympathetic response in me. I was young at the time when everyone read and was enthusiastic – or pretended to be enthusiastic – about the great Russian novelists. I read them, too. And admired them – only without anything that resembled real fellow-feeling or a sense of living in the world they described.

Intourist parked us at a hotel called the Savoy, as far as I remember. It was the most absurd place in which I have stayed, I thought at the time. It must have once been an elegant hotel – there was a series of dining rooms with walls excessively gilded and silvered and ceilings painted with frescoes of floating ladies dressed chiefly in clouds, roses, and cupids, mirrors high and low, some of them still whole. To get from our rooms to these dining-rooms we had to wander on an endless journey along corridors and back stairs, for now and then we would come to a passage blocked by a pile of debris from the walls or a hole in the floor. To me it looked as if the people who manage this hotel get an idea from time to time that here is a place where repairs had better be made. Here and there the walls were torn up so pipes of all kinds were laid bare – and with that the whole idea of repairs was given up so completely that nobody ever thought of removing the plaster which had been chopped off.

The lobby was outfitted with gigantic pieces of furniture, in all styles from the early eighties to *Jugend-stil*. And on shelves and tables, along stair landings, in hall windows, everywhere stood the most wonderful collection of the white figures of plaster, gypsum, or biscuit, or whatever the material was, of which most middle-class homes in my childhood boasted specimens. The girl with the guitar – I believe Mignon was her name – the lady in bathing costume, boys with dogs, and girls with a cat or a dove, Beethoven, Moses, hunters, horses, pairs of lovers in rococo dress and in medieval German garb, ladies in little or nearly nothing, they were all there. Involuntarily I got the idea that here were collected the treasures from countless liquidated bourgeois homes.

But the strange part was that all these things were relics from the homes of the bourgeois society I remembered from when I was a small girl; there was not one thing which was reminiscent of *my* generation, not to mention more recent times. And the feeling that the new Soviet Russia is the inheritor of a bourgeois past which I remember but faintly, of something which for us from Western Europe is a distant childhood memory – *that* I received everywhere in Russia. It was not only the fact that in not one of the homes into which I looked while I strolled along the streets hour upon hour during the evenings I was in Moscow did I see any article of furniture which did not belong to that far-away past – except the iron beds with which some of the rooms were crowded. (Not one furniture store, open or closed, did I see in a single place in Russia.)

But constantly I got the feeling – now in one way, now in another – that the new Russia is built, not upon the ruins of our time, the ideas of our time, but on the world of our grandparents. There was the contrast between the pretentious new buildings, the show places of the Soviet state – the subway's marble-covered station, the immense unfinished library, and other ambitious building projects which were not yet completed and looked as if they probably never will be – and then the indescribable filth, dilapidation, wretchedness in all the houses in which people *live*. That was the way the bourgeoisie throughout Europe arranged things when I was a child – with great show parlors facing the street, in which the family "received" its guests and collected all that money and poor taste could provide, to impress visitors. While it slept and begot and bore children in dark, miserable rooms in rear premises so gloomy and close that the air in the bedrooms did not get better, no matter how many windows one opened.

That was the time when prophets could still predict that the development of the capitalistic bourgeois society would inevitably end with all the wealth gathered in a few hands; the others would be propertyless proletarians, without the ability to protect themselves against exploitation, and the whole middle class would crumble away little by little and become one with this proletariat. Yes, God knows, also at home in Norway there were still many of my generation who believed it, because their parents and teachers had told them that was the way it would go. And then it was of little use that we others pointed to what was happening before our eyes – that it was the middle class that was growing. With lightning speed it produced a class which grew steadily broader, of directors and under directors, office personnel, technical experts, foremen, specially trained professional workers. *That* was the development. *It* revolutionized the old-fashioned individualistic capitalism. And it was to be this new middle class, composed of good and bad, of honest and unscrupulous people, that played the leading role when revolution did break out, at any rate in capitalistic countries. In the crises which accompany a depression or a war or anything else the bloodiest battles were to be between that part of the middle class which was still tied by economic interests to a restricted production machinery and those who were eliminated by a shrinking production machinery.

The books of tickets which we had been given by

Intourist contained also admission coupons for sightseeing tours with guides through Moscow. Hans and I did not use ours. The museums and "sights" of a city are worth while if one has time to stay some months. But if one's time is scant, I prefer to see the city itself. The streets, the people, the shops, the glimpses of people's homes in the evening, when the lights are on. Squares and parks where children play and lonely people sit on benches, the outlying sections through which one rides on the street-cars, until one catches a glimpse of the landscape in which the city lies and which it is swallowing up.

So I have not seen Lenin's mummy. But I have seen the queue which stood for hours and waited to get into the mausoleum. And I have seen the Red Square lie as barren as the steppes, when the mausoleum was closed – but along the outskirts of the square the river of people streamed. The side streets poured their tributaries into it, and people walked, walked, walked. I have not been down in the famous subway. But a time or two I tried to board the packed street-cars, with people hanging in clusters inside and outside. The street-cars leap and dance on the billowy rails, for the streets everywhere in Moscow are full of holes and humps; they look as if they had been broken up by freezing through many winters but had never been repaired. "Watch your step" – that applies in Moscow more than anywhere else. Breaking an ankle is an easy matter in a nest of paving stones which frost has piled on edge.

Hans and I walked the streets in Moscow, the four days we were there, all of the time except for the hours we spent in delivering papers and fetching them and getting our coupons exchanged for tickets on the Trans-Siberian Railroad. I do not believe there were more such formalities in Russia than elsewhere, but it takes five or six times as long for Russians to get anything accomplished. They rummaged and searched in piles of papers and pamphlets and railroad schedules, as if it were the first time they had laid their eyes on these things, for each new passenger who was disposed of. And before they dared to decide that two and two made four they had to consult their abaci.

Still Hans and I had ample time to wander about in Moscow. And I imagined, I could feel, there is something hypnotic in collective life, one loses oneself in a way when one moves with a stream of totally strange people with whom one cannot talk, whose faces tell one absolutely nothing. Not that people in Moscow looked unhappy (but I did not see *one* Russian who smiled, except the attendants on the Trans-Siberian Railroad). So they looked even less happy. The English word "stolid" is perhaps that which best describes the expression on the faces of Russians. But I confess I could not see any individual differences in persons in Russia. In Japan, for example, I do not think people are more alike than in any western European or American crowd. One sees handsome men and ugly men, wise and stupid, sensitive and brutal faces. One sees old women one would have been glad to know and old women one would not like to know. Even the young women in Japan, almost all of whom look charming, at any rate when dressed in kimonos, have an individual charm. Some have a regular and refined beauty, others look very common, but are sweet all the same.

To me, at least, the Russians seemed more homogeneous. In the cities nearly all the men were beardless, but unshaven, a grimy blue or yellow or red about the jowls. Some wore short trousers, some long, some were in shorts, some were dressed in light shirts open at the neck, some in Cossack blouses – sometimes with cross-stitch embroidery on the collar and belt. Some went naked to the waist and showed bare bodies, brown from the sun. But all seemed coarsely built, heavy-knuckled, with low brows, high cheek-bones, and large triangular noses jutting out from their faces.

The large, straight, projecting nose most of the women had also, and short, broad, strong-boned faces. Some had light hair, some brown, some red, but I thought all those I saw were alike. They wore thin cotton dresses – not too unattractive at a casual glance. But the material in these dresses was so wretchedly thin and sleazy that if I had dared, for example, to give my maids such goods for a dress, they would have been deadly insulted and would have informed me it was not worth paying anyone to sew, or taking the time to sew oneself, on such worthless stuff.

Meanwhile the Russian women, poor things, had put a great deal of work into sewing these miserable cotton materials. And the pathetic thing was, they must have had some western European fashion magazines, at first or second hand, to follow. So they had sewed up that flimsy cotton print into dresses of a kind of evening-gown style, with the whole back bare (saving a yard and a half of material), with small puff sleeves of strips of cloth which hung from the bare shoulders, covering the elbow. The skirts were short, of course, and I saw stockings on only a couple of beggar women – God knows why they had not exchanged them for food. All the others went barefooted, or wore short cotton socks, with canvas shoes or galoshes or bedroom slippers. In all Russia I did not see one woman with leather shoes on her feet.

The children were generally barelegged and dressed in washed-out little bloomers and nothing more. But they all looked well, brown-legged, and not thin enough to hurt. There were throngs of children and Moscow swarmed with young women who would soon present the state with more children. And it seemed that the Russians were happy to have children – the innumerable babies whom people carried with them were better cared for, were carried carefully and properly, were kept cleaner than anything else I saw in the country. Often it was the young man who carried the baby, the woman trudging behind with a bundle, or a package wrapped in newspaper. I saw some five or six baby-carriages, all in Moscow.

Now this was, of course, the middle of July, and it was blazing hot in Moscow. Every day we were there it clouded over during the evening – thunder rumbled somewhere in the distance, warm rain fell on the city of millions. And the heat became even more oppressive, heavy, and wet. As in a Turkish bath, heat steamed from the pavement, from house walls and narrow smelly rooms – the air was richly saturated with innumerable kinds of evil smells.

I had, naturally, read so many conflicting accounts of the Soviet Republic, heard from people who had been there of its glories and its wretchedness – what is seen depends here more than ever on what eyes are looking – I thought I should not be surprised at anything I saw. What surprised me, a little, at any rate, was the sameness of the picture. Here there was in truth no noticeable difference in people; that one must grant the Russians. The crowds in the outskirts of the city, the crowds in the heart of the city, wore equally flimsy clothes, were equally unkempt and frowzy-haired. In the houses which face the wall of the Kremlin and the old imperial riding school, people sat on the balconies around a samovar – the section must once have been the "elegant" quarter. Now these places were just as run down as all the other houses, and the women and men on the balconies as miserably clad as everyone else.

What I had had no previous idea of was the

stench in Moscow. So that was what made the most overwhelming impression on me. The fetid smell of cotton goods which has been washed again and again, but without soap, of women's unwashed hair, the smell of bedrooms closely packed with dirty beds, which emanated from each open window in the summer night. The smell of urine and excrement from the dirty yards, where a row of shanties in a state of near collapse did duty as outdoor toilets. And over the whole city the smell of things which rotted and crumbled and fell into ruin, the smell of woodwork eaten up with fungus, and walls with the mortar peeling off the stones, the smell of the black slime in the cracks between the pavement stones and the holes in the asphalt.

A peculiar ingredient in the symphony of stench was a greasy, sharp, and dreadful smell, as when oil rots and gives off poisonous acids – the smell of a kind of grease with which Russians oil their boots, but still the smell of the boot grease. But of course the soldiers had boots.

One thing about Moscow which reconciles you with much – in my eyes, at least – is the Russian people's evident love of flowers. The parks in the city were nothing to boast of – some sad little patches of green, some rows of ill-tended trees here and there on the broad boulevards which run through the city, on the immense open squares which stretch out into barren deserts, cut across by the streams of people. Parks in Russia look almost like the vacant lots one sees here and there in the crowded sections of Brooklyn. I saw no gardens around the houses anywhere. In the outskirts of Moscow there are still whole streets of nothing but old one-story frame houses, formerly single-family dwellings, each on its spacious lot, with old and sickly-looking trees and tufts of grass and weeds and refuse and scraps of paper strewed about. Those who live there seem to have neither the time nor the means – nor the desire – to do anything with their lots.

But in nearly all the windows everywhere in Moscow stood potted plants – often so many and so large that, they protected the rooms within from curious eyes, if that was the intention. Philodendron and rubber plants – they too reminded me of the eighties at home in Norway, they were the fashionable plants then. But many other potted plants also – and they all seemed to be thriving. When I was a child the old women used to say foul air and loving hands are what potted plants need in order to thrive. Perhaps there is something in it.

Flowers, too, were almost the only thing offered for sale on the streets of Moscow. Sweet William and summer chrysanthemums, hardy flowers which country people can have on a patch of land and need hardly care for – it was women from the villages near Moscow who stood selling them. The bouquets were not very fresh, many looked as if they had been brought back and forth many times. But there was always someone who bought them as well.

I am not one of those who imagine that people

who are fond of flowers must be fundamentally good. Even people who love animals can be either-or: some love flowers and animals because they like everything which lives and grows; some because they cannot get on with their fellow men, cannot care for anyone but themselves – a dog or a garden becomes a precious compliment to their ego. It is possible, as Rauschning tells, that Hitler loves his canaries and weeps when one of them dies. – But I happen to be very fond of flowers myself, and every evidence of the Russians' love of flowers that I saw gave me a comfortable feeling that perhaps we could have found a common meeting-ground if I had only understood one word of their language.

One feels so sadly stupid going about in a strange city where one cannot even understand the writing on signs and street-corners. So I determined, before we started out on the long trip across the continent, to be sure to buy a small Russian conversation book, so that I could at least teach myself the Russian letters and read the names of the stations along the way.

I secured the address of a kind of university bookshop which was open every day. And it was crowded with people – young and old, men and a few women, who poked about in piles of books, stood bolt upright completely absorbed in a book, or walked around in the shop, conversing in low voices. And that was, indeed, the only time I saw Russians reading. It is said that Soviet Russia has accomplished great things in the battle against illiteracy. But if all people have learned to read, it does not follow that they have acquired the desire to read. I never saw anyone buy a paper at the news-stands, nobody sitting on the benches in the so-called parks was ever reading a paper or a book. *Pravda* I saw high and low, but always used as wrapping paper. Nobody in the restaurant of the hotel ever read a paper as he ate. But this university bookshop was, as I said, populous. And quite well filled with books. Print and paper were dreadful – almost as in the German newspapers just before this war broke out.

To begin with, there was absolutely nobody in the whole shop who knew a word of anything but Russian. All those to whom I spoke seemed kind and helpful, it was only that they could not help me. They wandered around among themselves and talked Russian – now and then a man or a woman came over to me and made signs, here they had found someone who could – but then the new one knew no more than the others. They wrote notes and handed them to me – but of course they made me no wiser. Finally an old man appeared, and he actually knew a sentence or two of German. From a cabinet he brought me a book: *Wer lebt glücklich im Sovjet-Russland? (Who Lives Happily in Soviet Russia?)* it was called. But it contained no key to the mysterious Russian alphabet. –Before I left Moscow, however, I was given a small German-Russian text-book. It was intended for soldiers.

Hans had come to Russia with great

expectations. Like most young Norwegians he had been much occupied with the Communistic experiment and was ready to accept all of it which as a Catholic he could. His indignation over the reality, as we saw it, was almost comic. I had, of course, seen the poor and dirty and dilapidated districts in the slum quarters of, for example, Paris or South Shields – but in Moscow every place is a slum – and Hans has seen now the poverty-stricken districts in New York and Brooklyn. But at that time he had never been outside Scandinavia. So he had never dreamed that anything so filthy and wretched could exist. His horror was boundless when he learned that he must not drink unboiled water anywhere in Russia – a city of millions without safe drinking water. That was to me also, however, one of the most aggravating things about Moscow.

But it was the beggars especially who shocked and infuriated him. And it is true – below the masses of uniformly poor and neglected-looking people in Moscow we now and then had an unpleasant glimpse of a pariah population, people whom the system of government had placed outside the social order, who have no right to be wherever they may be, who have nothing to live on except the alms they can get by begging. And they seemed a concentration of misery, a good deal worse than the worst I have seen anywhere else. Pressed against a wall where the stream of people flowed past hung these bundles of rags, mostly old women, their skin a crusty black from filth and houseless living, their hair green from dirt or mold; some forlorn children begged, too. The boy shivered with sympathy and sorrow, and when we had given our last ruble note and kopek he demanded that we go home, "for I cannot bear to go past them without doing something."

That was also the only thing in all Moscow for which we could use our rubles. For there was literally not a thing in all Moscow which we could buy.

We saw innumerable beggars on Sunday when we drove out to a village, called Kolomanskaya, to the best of my recollection.

On a hill over the Moscow River, which here flows in a large bend, lie a group of old churches and a large monastery. The intention is to preserve the place as a kind of folk museum. The buildings have been allowed to stand there, practically empty of furniture, but I could not discover that any attempt is made to keep them in repair. An old wooden church from a northern village has been moved down here, however, and set up in a grove near the monastery, and a kind of stand has been arranged where we paid a half-ruble a person and got tickets to the whole grounds. We saw no sign of supervision; we could walk around as we wished. And it was pretty everywhere – large green knolls, poplar trees down by the river, quiet and sunny, and a wide view over the plain which spread out, bright with summer hues, with a scattering of small towns and new factories under a light-blue sky with drifting good-weather clouds.

The river was full of people who were bathing. – Later I discovered Russians bathe wherever there is water to get into – at the river banks outside the cities in Siberia, in brooks and ponds along the railroad line. Even in mere mudholes at villages there were always men and boys splashing and ducking. Perhaps it is only to cool off in the broiling summer heat that Russians jump in wherever they find water. Or it may be that they really do wish to keep personally clean, in spite of all the obstacles which conditions place in the way of such desires – overcrowded houses, dirty cities, toilets (if one can call them that) swinelike beyond imagination, lack of soap and preparations for keeping themselves free from fleas and lice. The half-naked boys and girls who walked up and down the hills at the bathing-places looked happier than people generally do in Russia. Many of them were carrying home bunches of flowers and rushes.

Beyond the monastery was what must have been the monks' orchard – many hundreds of apple trees in rows straight as a string. There were still signs that the ground around the roots of the trees had been kept open, the trunks whitewashed once upon a time. Now they stood straggling, dead, and ghostly white against the green hill. It is not only in Finland that the hard war winter killed fruit trees by the thousands; in the entire part of Russia through which I came I saw more dead than living apple trees.

One of the five churches in Kolomanskaya believers are still permitted to use – a large whitewashed building with blue-painted bulbous domes, from which the Greek crosses still point toward heaven, anchored by chains which once were golden. Along the high open staircase old men and women, mothers with small children, ragged youngsters, were sitting and lying, and all reached out a hand or a little tin cup. And most of those who entered gave them something, if only some copper coins.

The service was ended, but all the rooms in the church were crowded with people. They kneeled, crossed themselves, and kissed crosses and icons, moved on their knees from image to image. No matter how large the Russian churches look from the outside, their interiors are astonishingly narrow. The main room under the central dome is small but disproportionately high under the roof, and the painted screen which shuts off the chancel, all the side altars with their images, make it still narrower. Around the center room there is a labyrinth of small chapels connected by halls in which one can lose one's way. It is not strange that the Russians needed so many churches at the time when religion was a part of their everyday life. No individual church has been intended for large gatherings.

In one side chapel the people stood packed like herrings in a barrel. There was to be a baptism, and there were ten or twelve small baptismal candidates, each with his party. But Hans pulled at my arm:

"God help us, Mother, a child's corpse is lying there, too – and it has already begun to rot."

And it had. In the middle of the room stood a small coffin, covered with pink material. And in the coffin lay the body of a child, about six months old. It was dressed in white and adorned with cloth roses – the face swollen and turning blue-green. Someone had placed a wad of cotton under the nostrils to receive the dark fluid which oozed out. On a small altar at the foot of the coffin stood some saucers with cakes and a kind of sweetmeat. It was evidently the intention that the priest was to bless the food for the funeral guests.

It was, of course, dreadfully unhygienic, and the little dead child did its share in making the air foul. And still, in spite of everything, I thought this church was the most homelike and comfortable thing I had seen in Russia. After all the gray and somehow empty and flat poverty outside it was good see a poverty which at any rate had warmth and color, which took life and death solemnly, demanded consecration at children's entry into and departure from the world. So I did like the other people in the room – knelt and kissed the edge of a large picture of Christ which hung on a wall near the coffin. But I could not help thinking of bacilli and contagion.

We drove home through the village. I do not know whether it was the intention that it was to be part of the folk museum and that was why it had been allowed to keep its old-fashioned character. At any rate, all the houses were built in two long rows on both sides of a water-soaked road with deep ruts. It twisted its way under old rowan trees and poplars. The square wooden houses were silver-gray with age. On the one narrow wall which faced the road the windows and a small dormer window on the roof were encased by wide frames, coarsely carved in vigorous openwork patterns. Once upon a time these window-frames had been painted in gay colors – sky-blue, grass-green, bright red, white. An after-glow of something festive still lay over the old village; and there still grew in some spots by the houses hardy perennials or bushes, hollyhocks, sweet William, elder bushes, rose bushes, which bore a few flowers in the midst of the decay.

I am very ready to be convinced that these Russian peasant homes from the old times have never been ideal dwelling-places for people. Doubtless they were always too crowded, too leaky, too poorly isolated from the ground to be healthy. But I think here at any rate the new must have had something old on which it might have been worth while to build further. Elsewhere in the would we have long ago discovered that single family homes offer the best conditions for health, both physical and mental, that to children especially they offer inestimable advantages. So even if one wanted to experiment with collective farming, why not develop further the old village plan in the matter of housing workers? Again I was reminded strangely of old times when people in the West also imagined it was economical and progressive to pack families together in tenement buildings in crowded districts. Here again Russia apparently is trying to build the new on a foundation of ideas which the democracies have long ago discarded as unsuited to their purposes, as unfeasible in the light of what experience and science of the last fifty years have taught us.

2

Eventually the hour of departure struck. We had not been in Moscow more than four days. But it seemed a small eternity.

At the station we sat on our trunks and waited – for three hours. Some human wrecks, even more miserable than the others we had seen, slunk up to us now and then and begged. Young women worked as porters – but we had already become accustomed to seeing that the Russian women do all sorts of heavy work which we at home consider absolutely men's jobs. I wonder if this equality between the sexes in regard to the heaviest drudgery and the roughest manual labor prepares the ground for slave-state systems. Because in Germany it has always existed. In South Jutland, for example, from early times the boundary between the German and Nordic settlements has been clearly marked by the nature of the work done by women. Even when the language boundary had been erased, everyone knew that when people and cattle live together in one room (typical of the "Saxon" farm) and the women must perform the kind of tasks which the Danes consider man's work, the Nordics' land ends and Germany begins.

Trains came in and went out of the station. At length the train we were to take arrived, and so we started – five hours later than the scheduled time – on the nine-day journey from Moscow to Vladivostok.

Yngve and Alice had persuaded me to travel first-class on the Siberian railroad, so Hans and I had a compartment to ourselves. And in the other compartments of our car there were two occupants, or in some two adults and two children. The first afternoon passed in getting acquainted with the other occupants of our car: A Swedish engineer who was going to Japan to install some machinery in a factory there. An American doctor who had been with an ambulance in Finland. An English couple without children, and one with two children, a big girl and a small boy. An elderly Jewish professor and his stout, motherly, and comfortable wife – already they had long been refugees – now they came from Poland. A handsome young blond Norwegian, a dealer in furs who had fought during the entire war in Norway; now he thought, under German rule, his branch at least would be completely destroyed, so he intended to try his luck in America, where he had business connections. One of these connections – a New Yorker – was traveling with him. The American was half-Jewish, but had a Russian mother.

In the compartment next to ours was a young Norwegian-American theologian who had studied at Lund for a year and had planned a summer vacation trip to Hallingdal to visit his relatives there. Now, of course, nothing came of it – and unfortunately Hallingdal had suffered greatly in the war, we had to answer when he asked us. He shared his compartment with a man from South Africa who had accepted a professorship in zoology at an American university.

Between the compartments are attractive small washrooms, shared by two compartments. And the two American scholars equipped the washroom which we were to use with them with boxes and bottles full of disinfectants and preparations for fighting the vermin evil of Russia. They generously offered to let us use all their contrivances as much as we wished. Unfortunately it turned out that their liberality was wasted kindness, for there was no water in the washroom, then or ever in our time.

In general, the cars on the Trains-Siberian Railroad must have been the last word in train luxury when it was built early in this century. And exceptionally substantial – for after all I saw of Russian management I am certain that not the least thing had been done to keep them in working order, but they are still in good condition. The railroad is broad-gauged, the compartments roomy – but Americans who are used to Pullman cars must think the berths miserably narrow and hard.

Actually our journey through Russia and Siberia was not strenuous. It was only a matter of sitting still and getting dirtier and dirtier. The train force did its best to make us comfortable – and that the best was not particularly good was not their fault.

There was, for example, the man Intourist had provided as a kind of tour manager. "Graatass" (the gnome) we Norwegians called him. He was a small, grimy, brownie-like figure whose looks made one want to put him to soak in a tub of warm soapy water overnight and run him through many clear rinsing-waters before he was hung up to dry. He was dressed in a moldy-gray sports suit which was a couple of sizes too large for him. But he was eager to be helpful – came and brought us books from the library car, which this train boasts. For Hans he had hunted up some text-books of geometry and arithmetic, and looked a little disappointed when Hans was not very enthusiastic about this edifying literature. Geometry and mathematics have always been his poorest subjects. And to the lessons which Graatass tried to tempt him to study he had said an eternal farewell in intemediate school.

He wanted to entertain me with a novel by Gorky in German and *Wer lebt glücklich im Sovjet-Russland?* I had guessed that already: the army, if anyone does. I do not count the "big shots" of the party, – of them I know nothing except by hearsay. And one of the things my parents took particular pains to teach me is this: "When anyone tells you anything about anyone, you may be sure of one of two things – either it is not true, or else it is a half-truth, and that is the worst form of untruth."

Graatass could talk German, if not fluently, at least enough for everyday use. So I tried to ask him about this and that which I saw along the way. But he did not know much more than I; he was from Moscow and had never before been farther east than Sverdlovsk. But this time he was allowed to go with us all the way to Vladivostok. And it was really touching to see how happy it made him – because in Vladivostok he would see steamships, real ocean-going steamships. And until now he had never seen any boats except those which ply the Moscow River.

Then there was the porter who came and made up our bunks in the evening, and came again some time the next day and cleared away the bedclothes. He also was the typical small-sized Russian, with a face broader than it was long, and unbelievably dirty. His name was Vanya, as far as we could understand. And Vanya had narrowly excaped from paying dearly for the Russian uncleanliness. He had got a scratch over his right eye when he left Moscow; the next day his whole eye was dreadfully swollen, and in the crack between the eyelids the eye was blood-red, and discharged pus. It was easy to see that the man was really sick and had a fever. But in spite of everything he fussed and struggled with his work, doing as well or as badly as he could.

I washed out the eye and sore with a boric solution and tied a boric compress over it as well as

I could. Later in the day the American doctor woke up and took charge of Vanya's eye. After that he quickly grew better. Dr. D., incidentally, acquired a thriving practice little by little – before we came to Vladivostok everyone in the car, except me, had been his patient. The well-stored first-aid kit which Alice and I had prepared was nearly empty.

Vanya was endlessly kind and helpful to us all the way. He pretended not to see it even when we committed the two deadly sins which brought the rest of the train staff up in arms. One was that we shut off the radio, which chattered and raved almost incessantly from early morning until late at night – with a lot of Russian talk and in between a dreadful yowling of Merry Widow waltzes and ancient favorites. The other, and worse, sin was when we tried to pry open a window in the burning hot compartments. Graatass explained that it was because of the dust which drifted in and ruined the walls and carpet.

The carpet was, in fact, cleaned every morning. When Vanya had got the bedclothes out of the way, he came back with a broom in one hand and a glass of water in the other. He took a good mouthful of water and squired it over the floor, then he swept the carpet. I had read about this method of cleaning in one of the delightful works of Dr. Tode; that noble representative of the period of enlightenment in Denmark, at the close of the eighteenth century, in his fight for "the good of the greater number," writes zealously against this and other unhygienic practices.

It was really droll to see it in use. But I looked forward to the moment when I could throw the bedroom slippers I was wearing into the Pacific Ocean.

The country on both sides of the railroad line was beautiful, but extremely monotonous. From the Baltic Sea to Lake Baikal the whole continent was a continuous plain, sometimes faintly rolling, sometimes completely flat. Rivers and brooks with water like dark glass twined their way into the distance – it looked as if the water were standing still, it ran so slowly. All the villages were exactly alike – gray cottages of wood with the narrow side facing a road which looked as if people and cattle had worn this track across the land. Even in the largest towns we passed, most of the roads and streets we saw from the train were like this – wide or narrow tracks, not laid out according to plan, not built – the people themselves had tramped and driven them into existence; and after the thundershowers which fell almost every evening, the reflection of the sunset shone golden from a thousand mudholes in the roads. It looked beautiful, but it can hardly be healthful. The houses looked as if they had been placed at random – sometimes in a hollow in the field, where standing water gathered, so people waded in it to their ankles when they went in and out of the huts. Foundations they never had – at most they were banked with mud – nor did they have eaves-troughs or drainpipes; after the rain the water ran off the roads down into the pond in which the house stood.

Most of the villages were large, the buildings scattered without plan or order over an immense terrain. The cities looked like the villages many times enlarged. In some of the largest, however, there were blocks of factories, new and old, brick buildings that looked like tenements, and buildings with a certain official look, to judge by the style of their towers and domes and balconies, most of them dating from the close of the last century. But even in these largest cities the brick sections constituted only a small nucleus, surrounded by great stretches of village gray with gray wooden houses with gray shingle roofs of board, along gray, muddy roads over a gray, muddy plain.

No sign of gardens and trees by the houses, as in Kolomanskaya did I see again until we had come many days' journey eastward upon the plateau beyond Lake Baikal. In Russia itself and in western Siberia the ground around the houses was bare trampled ground on which weeds hardly grew.

Here and there in the outskirts of a village there was a small wooden church with a trace of whitewash. And once or twice, farther inland, we saw, usually on a hill, large churches with gilded bulbous domes and long convent-like buildings, surrounded by groves of trees and orchards of dead fruit trees. What they are used for now I do not know.

Cultivated land alternated with woods, mostly

birch and elder, a small pine wood or some larches once in a while. Along cart roads which lost themselves in the woods lay small piles of firewood, or two or three small haystacks of woodland grass. The pasture must be excellent in these light leafy groves – but I did not see a cow or a horse in the woods. In Norway or Sweden or Finland the farmers would have let out their young animals and milch cows by the hundreds, let the horses from the farms go here all summer, whenever they were not needed in the farm work, so they could keep spirited and healthy; and the clank of bells from all over the woods would have announced that the fresh wealth of the woodland pasture was being used to its full value. But, on the whole, one of the most extraordinary things, at least to us Norwegians, was that the Russians seem to keep so few domestic animals. All the horses I saw on the entire journey were of one and the same strain – originally a light riding horse, I should judge, a beautiful animal, small, with well-formed head and slender legs, and trim, small hoofs, when one saw horses running loose on a field in fair condition and free from galls and marks of sickness, as we saw them at some places in Siberia. With a herdsman rider they looked magnificent. But it was tragic to see these small horses in Moscow and every where else hitched to heavy loads – mere skin and bone, sway-backed, with bloated bellies and harness sores, as most of them were.

Now and then – not often – we passed a herd of

cows. And actually the Russian cows seemed to be collectively inclined – they always walked or stood packed together in a tight cluster, and preferred to stay on a strip of trampled clay ground even if there were a green knoll near by, and some clumps of trees and bushes. I never saw a Russian cow behave like our individualistic ones, which like to scatter, each seeking its own spot of grass, or the shade under the trees, or breaking through bushes or small trees to scrub off annoying insects. Now sometimes – not always – there was a herdsman with the cattle, once in a while a herdsman on horseback, so perhaps it was a habit which had developed with being herded through generations, this staying together in a tight cluster.

In contrast, sheep, goats, pigs, always appeared singly, or at most two by two, outside some of the huts. They seemed to be private property; the collective farms apparently do not keep small farm animals. Here and there a few hens tripped about or two geese swam round by a house door.

My impression is that Russians keep scarcely a hundred head of large livestock and practically no small livestock, where Scandinavian farmers would have kept about a thousand of each. – I know that at the end of the Czarist period Danish agricultural experts were called to Siberia to help the development of farming and to establish co-operative dairies of the Danish type, and that this enterprise progressed sufficiently for Siberia to export a good many dairy products. Of course it is possible that the land is better utilized elsewhere, but I do not think it logical that the sections along an important railroad line should be far behind parts of the country in which communication is primitive. On the other hand, in a totalitarian state the lack of communications may naturally encourage the individual farms to produce more, because the farmers may hope to keep more for their own use. But according to our Scandinavian ideas, Russia could be the richest country in the world – without plundering its small neighboring countries and laying barren through mismanagement and disorder what they have built up – if the Russians were half as able workers as the Scandinavians or the Finns.

Once or twice we went past a new collective farm. The large houses glistened yellow and fresh-timbered, with five or six chimneys on the roofs, and many doors. They looked exactly like the old workers' barracks from the beginning of the industrial age in Norway; there are still a few of them near factories outside Oslo. "Wolves' dens" they are often called. They have never been considered especially successful homes, and we had hoped to get them liquidated before too long. Now, after the invasion and bombing of our homes, I suppose Norwegians must for the present put up with totalitarian standards of living in regard to housing also.

I could not discover any signs of a Russian forestry service along the way. But of course the timber country was most beautiful left as it was, in its completely natural state. Often we went past forest glades, where, as far as the eye could reach, a purple-red carpet of fireweed – *Epilobium angustifolium* – lay bright and thick around the black stumps left by a forest fire. And now and then the leafy forest opened around great stretches of marshland – and over the swamp drooped shining willow bushes and birch, with tussocks of stiff grass at the edge, black water-holes, and farther out immense flats of quagmire, verdigris-green.

And a profusion of wild flowers blossoming everywhere – on the slopes along the railroad line, in meadow and field, on every sunlit spot in the woods, made it beautiful wherever we traveled. At first they were the same flowers I knew from home – bedstraw, bluebells, all kinds of boragewort, with shining blue flowers and shaggy green, white daisies and yellow daisies, and fireweed everywhere. The purple-red splendor followed us all the way to Vladivostok. I did not see it in Japan, but in America it appeared again, the flowers given way to clouds of the silky white down seeds which have spread the fireweed over the whole Northern Hemisphere.

As we approached Baikal new plants appeared, many of which we cultivate in the gardens at home – small lacquer-red lilies, masses of light-yellow day-lilies in the meadows. Every time the train stopped in the middle of open country – and it did so often, sometimes we stood in the woods or in a field and waited half an hour to meet another train –

the passengers swarmed out of the over-crowded compartments, where the Russians lay packed together on several tiers of shelves, in their own dirty mattresses and bedclothes. People threw themselves down on the grass along the railroad line, lay half-naked and let themselves be baked by the sun, or they ran into the meadows and picked flowers, flowers, flowers – whole lapfuls.

Once I had been out, picked a few day-lilies and some stalks of wild orchid. Vanya smiled and said something when he helped me up on the train. And in a little while he brought an empty seltzer bottle full of water and put my flowers in it. At that time we had not had anything to drink except tea, since before we came to Sverdlovsk. We took glasses of tea into the compartments in case we should get thirsty during the night, we brushed our teeth in tea. Drinking-water was not to be had. In this respect our Russian fellow travelers were better off, for there was usually an opportunity to get boiled water at the stations. But we had not provided ourselves with kettles and pails in which to fetch it.

We started with a supply of mineral water, but it gave out as early as the third day of the trip. And that was fortunate, Dr. D. assured us. He suspected the mineral water of being the chief cause of the many cases of violent stomach illness, which put one after another of the travelers flat on his back for several days.

The Danish engineer in the next car got sick when he saw that the portion of ham he had ordered was crawling with maggots. The Norwegian business man and the English children blamed it on the bedbugs – they had been so badly bitten that they got a fever. The others blamed the heat or the food – but it is certain that the health situation on the train did not improve after we had run out of mineral water.

I did not think the food was of the very worst. That is, had anyone offered us such food at home in Norway, we should have been highly insulted. But after four days in Moscow I had already reached the point where I thought it was splendid that we had food at all. And the black Russian bread was good – if one likes and is able to eat dark, sour bread. The eggs tasted like those I remembered from summer vacations in the country in my childhood, when we had found the nest of a hen who had hidden herself in order to found a family. The aunts decreed that they were too old for kitchen use, but we could eat them ourselves if we wanted to. And we did, with good appetites. The other passengers, who had no happy childhood memories linked with the taste of spoiled eggs, were less pleased.

All the food we were served was taken on board at Moscow; no arrangements had been made whereby new supplies could be taken on at places along the way. So the meat smelled and tasted worse day by day. Worst of all was the lack of vegetables – a little shredded white cabbage in a kind of meat soup was all there was. Instead of potatoes we got dark-gray macaroni cooked into a kind of porridge.

The dessert, cheesecakes, I renounced after the first attempt. They smelled – and presumably tasted – like the stuff babies belch when they have drunk too much milk.

There was a welcome addition to the menu when we had gone a way into Siberia. Each time the train stopped, a crowd of ragged children and women who wanted to sell berries swarmed up to the dining-car – one ruble for a small teacupful, delivered to us in cornucopias made out of old *Pravdas*. The berries were dirty and most of them unripe but the dining-car staff was always willing to cook them for us with a little sugar.

The steward or head waiter, or whatever his title was, was a tall, stately Russian who looked and acted like a grand duke in an operetta. Gay and good-natured, he ruled and lorded it over us all and kept those in the car who could understand a little Russian in a state of laughter, even when they tried to grumble about the food. And he grew no less impressive as his white jacket became blacker and blacker, and smelled stronger and stronger day by day, because the huge blond man also was melting in the heat. He had only one jacket. I happened to spatter grave on his sleeve the second day, and the gravy spot was the last thing I saw when we took a hearty farewell of our grand duke at the station in Vladivostok. Presumably his white jacket served also as a sleeping-garment – just as the entire hotel personnel at Vladivostok, I observed, slept in their uniforms on sofas and chairs or on the bare floor in all the halls and corridors.

Sonya, who scurried about with food and tea glasses, was small and dirty and not beautiful, but she must have had "it"; for that matter, we all liked her. She seemed to be brim-full of laughter; it overflowed every time anyone tried to talk to her or a man came near her. In one of the brochures from the train library we had read that one must not offend a Soviet citizen by offering to tip him; but there is, of course, nothing to prevent one's becoming someone's personal friend and giving him a gift, as from friend to friend. And it was truly a friendly farewell gift which we clubbed together to give the citizens of the dining-car. – Vanya would accept nothing, although what we offered him was also sincerely intended as gifts from friend to friend.

So, in spite of everything, the visits to the dining car were a pleasant change. The worst problem was to accustom oneself to the filthiness – gradually the tablecloths reached such a state that they stuck to your arm if you rested your elbow on the table. Dishes, spoons, forks – some of the passengers wiped each piece with a napkin before using it. But the napkin was no more reassuring, in my opinion. The blessed toilet paper from Sweden came to use here, too. I took in a couple of sheets and wiped off Hans's and my dishes and silver a little.

3

Very naturally the conversations in the dining-car to a considerable extent centered on the state of health in Soviet Russia. Now, none of us knew anything definite about it – a number of years ago they stopped giving out any statistics which can lead to reliable, or even unrealiable, conclusions about sickness and health, births and deaths in the Soviet Union. Friends in Moscow, who still took a rather optimistic view of the future development of the country, believed the Russian medical profession was sufficiently good so it would be able to fight eventual epidemics with considerable success. But most foreign doctors – Dr. D., for example – believed that would not be possible, in a country where not a single city or country town had water which can be drunk unboiled, where there is a shortage of soap, rooms are overcrowded everywhere, where the cities have no sanitation departments to speak of, and the majority of the houses are built on flat, undrained land. About the food situation we of course could not know anything definite, – people in general did not appear obviously undernourished, and there is supposed to be enough bread, and good bread. But a shortage of supplies exists everywhere and becomes catastrophic from time to time; last winter in Moscow there was for a long time no food to be bought by ordinary people except bread and white cabbage, which cost seven rubles a pound. There are so few clothes that in the winter people are forced to bundle themselves in everything they own; there can be no question of washing and changing. And last but not least, refuse is allowed to pile up everywhere, the smell of rottenness and decay filled the air wherever I went. And the toilets – to express oneself politely – were indescribable, unthinkable, if one had not seen and smelled them. The outdoor latrines in Moscow were dreadful, but we were to learn how much worse a modern water closet is when it is without water.

All the passengers in the cars had to brush their teeth and wash in the dressing-rooms, of which there was one in each end of the car. We stood in line morning and evening, in pajamas and dressing-gowns, our sponge bags and towels over our arms, and awaited our turn. But from time to time the water-containers in the car ran empty. And it might be a half day, once it lasted a whole one, before we came to a station where another locomotive drove up beside our train and a long hose poured boiling water into the containers again. The small washrooms between the compartments were never supplied with water. Vanya said "something" had rusted away in them. Fortunate was he who got a turn at the dressing-room when the newly supplied water was not so hot one scalded oneself, but deliciously warm.

Of one thing I became convinced on the trip through the Soviet: a population can live, and a part of it, at least, apparently keep healthy and able to work, on a standard of living which in the Scandinavian countries we should have considered fatal. What we had come to consider the lowest minimum per year and per person of fats and carbohydrates, of the various vitamins, of fruits and vegetables, in the totalitarian states only a thin crust of the ruling caste obtains. The totalitarian states do not care a damn about our ideas of the minimum of cleanliness and home hygiene necessary to keep the national state of health on a satisfactory level – and seemingly life goes its natural gait, after a fashion.

There is, of course, this difference: that in a country with three or four or six million inhabitants many factors combine to spur our efforts for the preservation of the precious lives and the protection of public health. It is not an insurmountable task to get a sufficiently large portion of a small and enlightened people interested in the fight for public health, so the work in Norway which was begun by private organizations – for example, the Norwegian National Society for the Prevention of Tuberculosis, the Norwegian Women's Nursing Association, and Norway's Red Cross, as well as a series of private enterprises in the cause of maternal hygiene and lowered infant mortality – soon, is looked upon as a community affair. The state steps in, takes over a number of the fields of activity started by the private organizations; and the organizations can exist and grow large while they widen their interests, take upon themselves pioneer work in community hygiene. Theoretically, at least, in a democracy all citizens have an influence, if not direct, indirect, on the state economy. In a small democracy it does not work in a long run for the governing to show complete indifference to the welfare of even the poorest groups; there is too small a distance between the governing and the governed, class distinctions are not so great, and movement from class to class is too rapid.

Norway had – before the German invasion – almost the lowest infant-mortality rate in the world. But Russia had a much higher birth rate than Norway – not to mention Sweden, where the birth rate is so dangerously low that it is obvious one must do all in human power to keep each child which comes into the world alive and in good health. Russia can afford to let children perish, to lose great numbers of adults, to hope that nature itself will in this way liquidate the weaker individuals and provide for the "survival of the fittest." Nazi Germany openly boasts that it is an integral part of the Third Reich's population policy – women must bear as many children as they can, nature and the conditions in the country will ensure that only the strongest and most hardy will grow up and propagate "the race." Mothers' irrepressible love for their weak and abnormal children in particular – that, too, is a "law of nature" – they refuse to recognize. It is, of course, at this time impossible to check the truth of the rumors of systematic murder of the weak, sick, or defective individuals in the Germany of today. If only half of what is said about that matter is true, then, for example, neither Swift, Newton, Darwin, nor Hans Christian Andersen would have had a dog's chance to live and carry out his life work. Of course, not Hitler or Goebbels either, or our own Quisling.

Presumably in the long run it will cost the totalitarian states dearly that they intentionally defy all laws of public hygiene which science in the last century has labored to establish. But in large thickly populated states – countries with 70,000,000 or 130,000,000 inhabitants – it may, I suppose, take some generations before the breakdown becomes complete. And before they themselves collapse, if they manage to keep the small, more advanced morally, and intellectually superior nations under the yoke long enough, they will have been able to destroy and decimate them so thoroughly that when they themselves are ended, the history of the white man or the glove is also ended. Black or yellow missionaries will perhaps seek out the remains of the white tribes in Eurasia or America, where they will be living as fellahs or nomads amid the ruins of our old world, to see if they can teach them a little of the new superior peoples' civilization and culture.

4

The Railroad stations on the Trans-Siberian Railroad were all built in the time of the Czars. It makes one believe there is something fundamental in the Russian nature which is unchangeable and dominates the picture of the realm, whether it is a despotism under a Czar or under a party which calls itself Communist.

All the stations have a long, imposing front facing the platform, and back of the façade there is almost nothing – a few rooms in a single row, almost empty of equipment. When we traveled there all the stations were full of ragged people who were sitting or lying on their sacks or rolls of bedding or on the bare floor – in the waiting-rooms, in the baggage sheds, around the walls of the station building, and far out on the open square ordinarily found behind the stations. They were people who waited – often for days – to get on a train. For though people lie like sardines in tins in the cars where ordinary Soviet citizens travel "hard," – that is to say, install themselves on the shelves with their bedclothes, packages of food, and tea paraphernalia, and often lie there day and night, as long as the journey lasts – there is no correspondence between available train facilities and the Russians' desire to travel.

To the moving stream of people on the streets corresponds a vast trek of Russians along the communication lines. Why do they travel? In the hope that somewhere else in this their world they will find better-paid work, more food, and perhaps better living-conditions, explained one of our traveling companions who knew Russian and had talked to some of them. Whole families were on trek – ancient grandparents with children and grandchildren, down to the newly born (who often looked miserable, in contrast to the babies in Moscow; the heat and air at the stations must have been enough to be the death of even the strongest and healthiest babies).

If it had not been for the thundershowers which came every afternoon and kept the ground around the stations continually muddy, those who lay outside must have had a little the better of the people in the waiting-rooms. The air there was horrible even for Russia, and permeated by the peculiar stench of the boot grease. Still I did not see that the wretched people at the station had boots, any more than others in Russia. Felt shoes and boots of braided birch bark became quite common, especially on the old people, as we got deeper into Siberia. But all the stations swarmed with soldiers, and *they* had boots.

But, in spite of everything, it was fun to jump out at the stations and mingle with the throngs of people on the platform. With bare legs in slippers, in nightgowns and pajamas, we bustled about in the early morning and made desperate attempts to buy cigarettes at station after station. The supply in the dining-car had given out on the third day, and in all Siberia there were no cigarettes to be bought, until we came almost to Vladivostok.

Signs – which I could now spell out – announced that here was a railroad restaurant, here a stand with newspapers and postal cards, here a lunch counter, here a shop with souvenirs. But none of these had a thing to sell, except the souvenir counter, which at some of the larger stations offered a selection of toys – Teddy bears and rag dolls and picture books of the simplest type. Whether it is a part of the Five-Year Plan which is being carried out – having toys for their children one of the few things Russians are able to buy – I do not know. I began to suspect that it was rather a trade agreement with the Nazi partner which explained why Russia was so relatively well supplied with toys of the cheapest quality.

The Soviet had brought the stations up to date by beautifying them with immense placards with inflammatory slogans, gigantic pictures of Stalin, Molotov, other Soviet heroes. A light-gray statue of Lenin – everywhere the same one – adorned the little lawn in front of the station. For there were lawns before many of the stations, small, with the hardy flowers which can live without being tended.

In old times it was always said that the Russians were a people with marked creative gifts, love of color, a strange, exotic, and refined taste. And even a person who, like me, has never been particularly enthusiastic about the samples I saw of Russian arts and crafts can remember that Russian products meant rich colors, bizarre patterns, something luxuriant and strangely foreign. The folk costumes were ornate, with a kind of hierarchic cast; they reminded one of liturgic robes of some strange cult. It may have been only a small portion of the country people – and more prosperous – who had such costumes, and *one* costume presumably served its owner for a lifetime and was handed down to the children; it is not likely that the products of Russian handicraft were common possessions. But in some places in Russia there must have been a love of color and what delights the eye – a flowering of beauty according to the people's sense of beauty.

So far as I saw, there was not a spot as large as a pinhead left of all this now. Uniform ugliness, faded and colorless and worn out, ruled the scene along. Now, the theaters in Moscow, which are said to be the inheritors of this Russian tradition, were not open when I was there. My son and some of our youngest traveling companions saw a performance in Vladivostok, but it seemed, like everything in Vladivostok, to be gathered from the scrap-heap: old actors (I saw the prima donna the next day in the dining-room; she was certainly older than I, and dreadfully crosseyed), the settings cast-offs, and the musical comedy they presented was *The Dollar Princess!*

The propaganda material which has been spread over the country for years is indescribably hideous – signs and placards and red paper streamers which are put up on holiday occasions and allowed to hang until they rain down. Icons of the various heroes which have been presented to the people for worship at the various stages of seizures of power and liquidations of the regime since the revolution would make one believe, if one did not know better, that they had been set up by counter-revolutionists to blacken Lenin, Stalin, and others in the eyes of the people. Compared with them, it was a noble and distinguished form of art which was provided by the jobless itinerant housepainters who in my childhood used to come to the kitchen door and tempt our maids to order "handmade" enlargements of photographs of father and mother and the sailor lad to whom they had been engaged. It looks as if this artistic opium, which the rulers for more than twenty years have forced down the throats of the people – together with poverty and filthy conditions – has lulled the Russian sense of beauty and color into a deep and dreamless sleep, or killed it – if it is possible to kill the artistic gift in a people which has had it. Which I do not believe.

As we gradually got deeper in Siberia, the picture became, in spite of everything, a little less monotonous. We passed country towns which looked a little less destitute and forlorn than most – here and there a village where there was a little enclosure with beans and cabbages, a currant bush or two, or an apple tree by the huts; a tethered calf or goat grazed near the house door. We saw also, sometimes, houses where the carved window-frames had recently been given a touch of red and green paint. One morning we passed a station where a woman stood selling warm *piroshki*. And at each stopping-place women and children swarmed up to sell blueberries and raspberries.

But beggars swarmed forward also each time the train stopped, and it was food they asked for. Children crowded around the entrance to the dining-car and called for bread. And they crammed down greedily whatever Mr. G., the New Yorker, gave them. They were misshapen from rickets, many of these children; from out their rags protruded ugly chicken-breasts and the rows of knobs in crooked, humped backbones. Legs and arms like matches, with large knobby joints. On the whole, however, we received the impression that people in Siberia were even more poorly dressed than in Russia, but that in part they lived better.

And we had glimpses of a deeper misery and human suffering, which hid itself beneath the surface of a uniformly gray and grimy but still certainly quite endurable everyday life.

One morning in the gray dawn we stood at a station a little east of Lake Baikal. A train came in on the track beside ours, large ironclad cars, with tiny iron-barred windows. Behind every window we could discern a soldier with a poised bayonet. "Prison transport," it was whispered. Then our train left, just as the other stopped.

We came to the Taiga in the middle of the night – a dark, steamy, sweltering night. We were exhausted and half-sick after having perspired through a broiling day which ended with a usual violent thunder and a down-pour late in the afternoon. On the side-track stood a train of ironclad cars, and now in the night, when there were dim lights behind the barred windows, we could see that the soldiers stood on guard in a narrow corridor; back of them there was also an iron wall. The soldiers smoked, and squeezed themselves tight against the windows to catch a breath of cool air, if it were possible.

Six or seven cattle cars followed the iron cars. The prisoners had been allowed to open the large sliding doors a little. Men, women, and children – large and small – were sitting and lying tightly packed together in the cars – there was a little light in them. And the station lamps shone on the guards who stood watch along the train.

Taiga means "wilderness out of which no road or path leads," said Mr. G., the American-Russian fur-dealer. The best pelts, marten and ermine, used to come from the primeval forests of the Taiga.

In comparison with the other Soviet citizens the soldiers were well dressed, with boots, caps, and uniforms which seemed to be of better material than the cloth Russians can generally buy, even if they did not look like really good material, shoddy mixed with a great deal of cotton. They evidently had cigarettes in abundance – an article which was not to be found in Siberia at the time of our journey. And there were swarms of soldiers all along the railroad line. We saw barracks and flying fields with planes on the ground and in the air at all the larger and many of the smaller towns. A great many of the westbound trains we met carried soldiers and war supplies.

The second Sunday we were in Soviet Russia we passed some small towns far toward the east. (The seven-day week had been restored just before we came to the country, to the great satisfaction of the people, it was said.) The free day was celebrated with a kind of military parade at athletic fields outside two of the towns, and there were quite large gatherings of people at the exhibitions. Otherwise the athletic fields we saw here and there in Siberia lay as deserted and empty as the quagmires in the forest. But it is true, of course, that the temperature was not conducive to sports events.

It has been predicted that if the Nazi government in Germany some day should fall and the German people threaten to escape from the party's stranglehold, the German army leaders would probably choose to put themselves at the head of a "communistic" revolution. After all I have seen of conditions in Russia, I think that is the way it will be likely to go, if the Nazi regime some day begins to totter. In a totalitarian state, whatever it may please to call its system of coercion, the army will always be the privileged portion of the people. So it would be a way out for the German army if it should feel that the situation began to threaten the position of power which it has held from the time of the Empire through the Third Reich – to call themselves communistic. It would give Germany a pretext for taking the great "communistic" conglomerate of

Soviet republics and half and wholly Asiatic peoples in Russia and Siberia under their "protection," helping it to utilize the infinite natural resources which the Soviet has still scarcely begun to develop – and for whose benefit it is easy to imagine, Soviet Russia would then have only the choice between submitting, and giving up all pretensions of being a communistic country – admitting openly that it is a nationalistic and imperialistic state system, ruled by a clique under the thumb of Josef Stalin.

The war in Finland had undeniably given the world ground for doubting that the sums of money and the suffering and deprivation which had been extorted from the Russian people to create a large and modern Russian army deserved to be called effective investment of capital. The fierce fight to defend their own country has proved to the world that the Russian army is a vastly more formidable adversary than was expected by anybody, probably the German warlords included. But whether Stalin's Russia would be willing to go on fighting Germany's *Wehrmacht* after it has torn down the Swastika and raised the sign of the Hammer and Sickle still remains to be seen.

And whether Russia chose one position or the other, the German dream of German domination of the world would gain an indefinitely extended lease of life. Communists of long standing and in all countries and all parts of the world, impatient, their ideas confused, and pathological agitators wherever democracy's obvious weaknesses have been glaringly illuminated by incendiary bombs and flaring danger signals, would line up behind Kaiser William's and Hitler's war machine, when it mustered under a red flag, and with frenzied zeal help it to fulfill the age-old German dream of Germany's triumph and the annihilation of Western, Christian, and democratic civilization in a German *"Götterdämmerung."*

5

The train came to Vladivostok on schedule, in spite of various delays – as the day before, when we had to stand and wait several hours while a gang of railroad laborers, mostly women, worked to clear away the wreckage after a railroad accident. What remained of the burned railroad cars lay in the fields on both sides of the track, and a part of the slopes on the sides was torn up. But we made up the lost time and completed the trip in the scheduled nine days.

It was twilight, and we were let off at a badly lighted station, where we had a chance to wander about and wait for several hours. Graatass explained that it was the automobiles which Intourist was to send – they had not come, and the hotel was at the other end of the town. So we walked around.

I looked in the waiting-room windows – the everlasting closely packed crowd of dirty people who sat or lay, silent and patient on their dirty bags of bedclothes, the same rancid smell. – But directly under one of the windows sat a little girl I could not take my eyes off of. My own daughter was sick from her second year until she died, at the age of twenty-three, and the little Russian girl resembled her in a quite strange way. Under the tightly tied white kerchief a pair of wide-open gray eyes looked out of a waxen-white narrow face, with the strange patient expression of a child who is accustomed to suffering.

Finally I asked the Jewish professor's wife to talk to her. The child sat huddled together on her bag of bedclothes; her father stood beside her, a large ruddy-faced man with a tousled dark beard, dressed in an ancient military coat, held together by a bit of rope. But he was very willing to talk to us about his little girl.

Her name was Oleha and she was twelve years old. Yes, she had consumption, – had been very sick, the last year she had spit blood every once in a while. But now she would surely soon be well, because she was to go to a people's sanatorium. At Krim. He himself was to go with her as far as Moscow, and from there Oleha would be sent to the south; and there all consumptive patients got well, he had heard –.

He thanked me, very happily, for my gift to Oleha, though God knows how he would manage to buy "something good" for her along the way. At any rate, he promised to buy berries for her at the stations. And Oleha gave me her hand – it was like taking the foot of a dead chicken, cold and fleshless.

The evening was sultry, but the child's cheeks were clammy with cold perspiration when I touched them.

I can hardly believe that she reached Moscow alive – with Heaven knows how many waits on the way, in overcrowded stations, where she and her father would have to wait for a train to come which would have room for them so they could roll out their mattresses on one of the shelves. And meanwhile she must have had the chance to contaminate so many of her fellow travelers that there would be enough to fill another sanatorium.

Next to the glimpse into the hell of the prison train Oleha was the worst I saw in Soviet Russia.

Eventually Graatass came and drove us like sheep up and down the stairs and out on the square in front of the station. The automobiles from Intourist had come, but there were just two five-seaters, so they had to take us in several trips. Finally, however, we found refuge at the hotel.

I had looked forward to having a warm bath. At the hotel in Moscow I had bathed, though the room and tub looked repulsive; but I gathered all my courage and also forced my son to be courageous. – One glimpse into the bathroom of the hotel in Vladivostok was more than enough – I preferred to keep the dirt I myself had collected on the trip through Siberia rather than to exchange it for that of other people. All the water-pipes of the toilet had been rusted away completely, certainly for more than a year and a day.

Again the dining-room was faded gold and mirrors and past grandeur and glory. And in the midst of the decay a row of rubber plants in large tubs shone resplendent – beautiful well-cared-for specimens, the handsomest I have seen. The next morning I saw one of the maids wash the great shiny leaves – the only thing which was kept clean in the whole establishment.

The hotel was full of refugees who were waiting for the *Harbin Maru,* the ship on which we also were to sail. They informed us that this place was a regular zoo as far as insect life was concerned – fleas, head lice, body lice, clothes lice, bedbugs – all kinds were represented. Did we have anything to use against them?

The Jewish professor's wife had sabadilla vinegar and insect powder; she divided them up and instructed us how to use them. My poor son Hans grew pale and stiffened with horror. In the twenty years he has lived he had never yet seen a louse, although he had gone to public schools in the city and in the country, and on walking trips and ski trips in the mountains, had slept in all sorts of shacks and huts. Hardly even a flea, though we have always had dogs and cats at home. In my earliest childhood it would still happen in Norway that children had "animal life." But now we had practically liquidated them; on the flight northward and in Sweden, when I slept night after night in shacks and trawlers and huts, in hay and bedclothes which workmen had used the week before me. I never remembered that anything like a louse exists. Nor was I ever reminded of it. The Germans have brought them back in hordes now.

While Hans stood in the background with the bottle of vinegar and a package of cotton, I killed the bedbugs I found on our beds and in the nearest neighborhood, and advised Hans to lie on top of the bed with his overcoat spread over him. (I do not think any Scandinavian could have managed to creep down in those hotel beds.) It was bad enough to sleep on them in the smell the bedclothes under us gave off as they began to grow warm. We got on fairly well. But many of our travelling companions were so bitten up that they had a fever.

And we were informed that we would have to stay at the hotel another night. The *Harbin Maru* was behind schedule. Graatass announced that he would take us out on a sightseeing trip during the day, to console us. But it turned out he could not procure cars. We had to walk, under his leadership. There was a museum in the town, and then there was the harbor with the ships. It was heartless of us, I suppose, to request the museum – he was so eager to see the ships. But at any rate we went to the museum.

Compared with Vladivostok, Moscow and Omsk and Irkutsk and Chita and all the other Soviet cities we had seen were almost well regulated and clean. Vladivostok is beyond description; one must have seen it to believe the way it looks. And having seen it, one still does not believe it – one imagines one's memory must be playing tricks.

It is supposed to have about one million inhabitants, and there is nothing wrong with the site – the city is built up along low heights around a wide and beautiful bay. Most of the imports from the United States and Japan go by Vladivostok – endless lines of freight cars go west from the city many times a day. And large quantities of wares are piled up on piers and open squares and along the streets – wherever they happen to be dumped. It looked as if they were left lying there until they went to rack and ruin. We passed mountains of radiator parts, of the type used in Europe in my youth; they were rusted together into great rufous mountains of scrap iron.

In the time of the Czars the city had a university. Now it is moved to Sverdlovsk, near the boundary toward European Russia. The museum was a memorial of the university era.

There was a small "Revolution Museum" with pictures of the men from 1918 on, some inartistic paintings of blood-drenched battle scenes, some pictures of labor demonstrations and idyllic family scenes (style: Sunday-school papers), and a series of caricatures of Japanese soldiers, vulgar and humorless in execution. That was that.

Then there was a gallery of paintings. Some hundred remarkably indifferent pictures, which looked as if they had been collected from disrupted prosperous homes where the owners were more interested in the gold frame than what was inside it. And two good small landscapes which told that the painters had studied in Paris or thereabouts some time in the eighties. In a dark corner of the stairway hung some icons, a few of them good.

The museum of natural history must have been good at one time. It was not much larger than one of the collections all larger schools in Norway usually have, but it was wholly devoted to the animal life, fisheries, and bird life of Siberia. It was in a sad condition – the fishes were split open so that the stuffing oozed out of them, the birds molted feathers, and the fur-bearing animals were badly moth-eaten. But it was touching to see the Russians – often father, mother, and three or four children – wander about and gaze at the exhibits, so keenly serious, all devout.

The ethnographic exhibit was like the one of natural history – small, interesting, but miserably kept up. We were reminded that innumerable Mongolian tribes and primitive cultures live in Siberia. Along the railroad line we had scarcely seen a Mongolian face, although some of the time we had traveled quite near the border of wholly Mongolian country.

At last the day dawned on which we were to get out of the Soviet paradise. It began with a near cloudburst. It is said there is rain in Vladivostok 360 of the 365 days of the year. I stood in my window for a quarter of an hour and looked at the queue which waited outside a small shop opposite the hotel; it had been opened in the morning, but I do not know what it had to sell. There was a kind of holiday in the city, and the people had dressed up as well as they were able. Some of the women had even had their hair dyed, for the water from their bare heads ran red-brown down their poor naked backs. I was curious to see how many umbrellas I could count. But I discovered only one, carried by an old man. And then there was a little girl who paraded with a child's rose-colored parasol – and imagine her pride! There were some two hundred people in the queue, and they stood and got as wet as drowned cats.

Meanwhile the young Norwegian fur-dealer came in, all excited: there were some people on a roof below his window, and evidently they were going to repair it. That we had to see – the only case we had ascertained of Russians' intending to repair anything.

The roof needed repairs badly. Flaps of corrugated iron, flaps of roofing paper, and rotted fragments of wood fluttered in the gusts of wind and rain. But the men on the roof had something other than repairing to do; they rigged up a large signboard: a picture of young citizens, men and women, with tetanus smiles on their faces, saluting a Five-Year Plan for the electrification of the Soviet Republic. That was what they were celebrating today, explained Mr. G. And a Frenchman at the hotel told us that a workman had asked him if people in Europe were acquainted with electricity, which Lenin had invented to help the Russian proletariat. I thought a Five-Year Plan to provide people with umbrellas would have been appropriate in this rain-hole called Vladivostok.

Then the automobiles came which were to take us to the place where the passport and customs offices were located. I stowed most of the clothes I had used on the train in the clothes-closet in my room – certainly no laundry in the world could rid them of their Soviet smell. And they would surely be of use to whoever found them.

The customs office was one of the cleanest rooms I have seen in Russia – fortunately, as it turned out that we were to be there most of the day. And when the hour approached five in the afternoon we began to regret that we had not followed Graatass' advice and taken a lunch with us from the hotel. At the hour of departure we understood that Russian food is at least better than no food at all.

The document from the Russian Minister in Stockholm worked again, so I escaped opening our trunks. I was only instructed to leave our rubles, in exchange for a receipt; if I ever return to Russia I can get them back. And I had only eighty-odd. Now I regretted that I had not given Oleha all of them.

For the other passengers the customs inspection was a needle's eye to pass through. There was not a thing in their trunks which was not taken out and searched – even spools and balls of yarn in the ladies' sewing-boxes were inspected thoroughly.

Briefcases, books, and everything called paper it took an endless time to go through. Everything was finally placed in charge of the one customs officer who knew German and even a few words of English, but no other languages. Some Polish workers, American citizens on the way to the United States after a visit to the old country which had ended in tragedy, had to hand over their prayer-books and rosaries. One of the English women had a diary, which she had kept for two or three years; she had also made notes during the trip through Siberia, and so it was confiscated.

But everything comes to an end. Finally we were put into the cars again and driven to the steamship pier.

That gave us our last impression of Soviet Russia. A wooden wharf so rotten that they had been forced to moor it with an ingenious system of beams and chains which were fastened to the roof of a house on shore. Of the piles which supported the wharf more were missing than left standing – one was reminded of rotten stumps in a row of teeth. The ship lay beside a pontoon of old barges, and to reach this we had to balance ourselves on a highly unsafe-looking old landing-pier, over coal-black water which stank worse than all the other stinking things in Russia. The water at the wharfs in a town is usually dirty and evil-smelling, but the harbor water in Vladivostok suggested most strongly the contents of a septic tank.

But the *Harbin Maru* lay at the wharf, handsome

and shining. Japanese sailors in spanking fine uniforms and cabin-boys in shining white jackets which they did not use as sleeping-costumes looked down at us from the railings. And through the portholes in the side of the ship we looked into a galley where the most enchanting row of teapots hung sparkling under the ceiling.

To come onboard the *Harbin Maru* was like a fairytale. Clean cabinets with clean berths, tiled bathrooms with quantities of boiling water, a dining-salon with gleaming tablecloths and china and silver, fruit on the table – was it strange that we wanted to like the Japanese, to try to believe of them that it is probably not the people, it is probably only a clique that is responsible for the policy of conquest and the war in China, for Japan's imperialism and its cynical claim of dominion over the peoples of eastern Asia. One becomes prejudiced in favor of the Japanese when one has seen only Russian ways for more than two weeks – and then one is interrupted in his attempts to make a kind of toilet by an obliging Japanese steward who smiles and announces that if the young man and the lady wish to bathe, they may do so now. – And the young Swedish woman who is on the way to Peru with her husband, an Austrian Jew, comes in crying and half-hysterical with joy because her small boy has eaten a fig and an orange and is so happy about his nice, clean bed. The child had had a Swedish nurse during all his four years of life; he got quite sick from the filthiness in Russia, and could not eat sour bread and spoiled eggs, did not understand why mamma could not get him milk and fruit, which he was used to having. She had been afraid of losing him, too, – "and, you know, my parents and sisters and brothers I shall probably never see again, for of course I do not know if we can ever come back to Sweden." But now it seemed the boy was out of danger.

Back of us lay Vladivostok, a horseshoe of lights which were mirrored in the coal-black water. And the *Harbin Maru* stole carefully out through the mine-field.

RETURN TO THE FUTURE

Japan En Passant

 No, it is difficult not be partial to Japan and to the Japanese when one comes from Russia.

Rashin in Korea was the first port at which we touched. I had heard revolting stories about Japan's activities in Korea – most recently from the Swedish engineer, who had frequently been in the Orient. He did not have much good to say for the Japanese, but so much the more for the Koreans, whom he called honorable, proud, liberty-loving people. With a certain satisfaction he called our attention to the fact that the Koreans walk as we do; the Japanese have a peculiar, shuffly, stoop-kneed walk, because they are accustomed from childhood to walking on wooden slippers which hang on the foot by only a strap between the great toe and the other toes. The Koreans' footwear resembles most closely a kind of moccasin. And they are taller, carry themselves erect, their coarse-featured faces generally have a serious, dignified expression. The women's dress is beautiful; the young girls wore a kind of silk blouse with raglan sleeves, tied over the breast with a bow of silk ribbon, the ends of which hang far below the waist. There were many of them down on the quay. And here in Rashin all the Japanese women, and many of the men handsome and dignified in their dark, quiet kimonos, with the black silk scarf draped about the hips, and with small fans in their hands.

The morning fog hung low, so of the landscape in which Rashin is situated we saw only green slopes bare of trees, with small reddish-yellow footpaths leading up into the mist. Most of the city itself lay behind one of the hills. Along the bay were large new wharfs of brand-new whitish stone and cement, with large new warehouses so glisteningly neat and fine that I have never seen a harbor in Europe which looked so polished and trim and beautifully clean as this one.

Coal barges lay alongside the *Harbin Maru,* and half-naked coolies carried up the coal in baskets on their heads. So it took time to get the barges emptied. But the engineer said human labor is so cheap here that it pays the ships to load coal in this primitive way. Once the workers had a recess down on the quay; they ate some strange green, stringy stuff, some sort of fermented leaves, with chopsticks. But they all washed their hands in a tub of water which was standing there before they began with their food bowls.

And those of us who had not been in the East before did not tire of watching the life on the wharf. The Japanese swarmed on and off the ship, and down on the wharf more people were constantly coming. The young women – many with open paper parasols – wore summer kimonos of light, often half-transparent cotton goods, gray-green, gray-blue, rust-brown, but in contrast to the subdued colors of the dresses was the multi-colored large patterned silk belt, the obi, always selected with the most refined sense of color combinations. Even the unusual walk seems graceful, as long as they wear Japanese costumes, with small snow-white socks and lacquered sandals of wood on their feet; when they wear European dress it makes a very different impression. Their faces were painted white and rosy-red, they greeted one another with deep bows and beautiful smiles, they tripped along behind the men when they were accompanied by men, and they carried all the hand luggage. Sometimes a baby in a harness on their backs. And one wanted to steal the babies, they all looked so sweet.

On board the boat I had already noticed indications that in Japan the man is the head and master of the family, even when he is as young as my son Hans. The waiters turned to him with the menu, served him first, presented him the bill. It was even more evident when we came to Japan, most evident of all at the temples in Kyoto, where the temple servants and guides led him around, showed and told him – and expected me to trip along behind the youth and keep silent.

Dr. D. traveled third-class on the boat and invited us down to see the quarters there. Over three hundred Japanese, men, women, and children, were lying or sitting in small stall-like compartments slightly raised above the floor of the immense room. It was the air down there that the doctor wanted us to try – it was entirely clean and fresh. But then the people there were busy washing themselves all evening – in the weak gleam of a lantern in the hall into the sleeping-room swarms of naked people hurried between great tubs of steaming hot water, they scrubbed themselves and one another, poured tubs of water over themselves, so the whole scene disappeared from time to time in billows of steam. If one counts cleanliness a moral quality, the Japanese should be one of the world's most virtuous people. I believe people in the Middle Ages were more realistic: they considered cleanliness, not a virtue, but a choice pleasure, and mighty lords of the Church, who themselves went dirty and louse-ridden in order to fight against the temptation of pride and luxury, donated baths on a large scale to poor people, who were not subject to the same temptations, but, quite the contrary, needed to strengthen their self-esteem and to luxuriate in a bath-house and all its attendant services. The respective moral qualities of the Russian and the Japanese peoples apart, it is considerably more pleasant to associate with the Japanese, with their always freshly washed bodies and always freshly washed clothes, than with the dirty and smelly Russians.

And the first view we had of Japan was quite enchantingly beautiful. Tsuruga, the little town on the east coast of Honshu, the main island, lies at the inner end of a fjord surrounded by forest-clad, peaked mountains. I had always imagined that the

Japanese color prints of landscapes must be strongly conventionalized. Of course they are, but it is a conventionalization of Japan as it is in reality; the artists have searched out the characteristic features of Japanese nature and reproduced them so that their art depicts the country more truly than any so-called "realistic" painter could have done.

A steep cliff, up the sides of which climb forests of dark pine trees and here and there delicate-leaved maples. A fragile wooden bridge over a mountain crevice –the brook gushes downward, and in the hurrying stream a weeping willow moves its pliant pale-green twigs. On the other side of the crevice lie some small houses with straw-thatched roofs and balconies borne up by wooden posts. A company of half-naked coolies with hats like mushrooms strain up toward the cluster of houses, where a lovely young kimono-clad lady stands on a balcony and dreams over the scene. Dots of fog around the mountain tops remove the picture from the background and the view at the sides, so the little set piece of Japan becomes something dreamlike and fragmentary. This is the way it looked at the bay of Tsuruga.

We came in early in the morning of the third day of our journey. Over the little town circled some strange large birds, like birds of prey, with ragged wings. When they alighted on the top of a telephone pole they looked like something midway between sea-eagles and vultures. There were a great many of them over all the cities in Japan which we saw. And we were told that they are protected, because they help to keep the cities free from refuse. That the Japanese keep themselves and their houses clean does not prevent them from throwing the refuse from their housekeeping wherever it happens to be convenient – over the garden wall, out in the gutters. And the shaggy gray birds of prey swoop down and eat up fish-bones, turnip peelings, the refuse from thousands of kitchens.

The customs and passport office sent people on board. And though they are a good deal brisker in their motions than the Russians, precise and businesslike, the inspection took almost as long a time. Each passenger was questioned both long and thoroughly about why he had come to Japan, how long he was to stay, if he had secured the necessary boat reservations to continue his journey.

One of our traveling companions, an artist in ceramics from Prague, was not permitted to go on shore. We had all liked the quiet, serious man. He accepted his fate very quietly now, but he confessed that he did not know what would become of him. There was no place where he had a right to be, and he had but little money. The *Harbin Maru* was to lie at Tsuruga two days; for so long he could stay on the boat, but after that – We promised to try to do what we could for him in Kobe, but that was of course a poor comfort for the man from Prague. He stood on the middle deck and waved at us as we drove to the station; it was a sad ending to that part of the journey.

The long streets in Tsuruga through which we drove seemed to us a horn of plenty. Open shops with overflowing sidewalk displays of foods, fruit, and vegetables resplendent with color, multi-colored streamers painted with Japanese letters, beautiful small wooden houses roofed with shining, gray-glazed tiles, flowering oleander bushes against a background of dark pine trees in the gardens, flowering vines and dwarf trees in tubs by the house doors. And the people who clattered along the street on their wooden slippers had time to stop, to greet one another and converse; the women stood outside the shops, leisurely and unhurried, fingered the wares, could choose and reject. If Tsuruga did not look like a picture of the blessings of peace – ! In spite of war in China and all that.

And the compartment was clean and attractive, and the windows were open on both sides; we were actually allowed to have a through draft. We rode in a valley along a small, clear river. At some places the railroad track runs close under the mountain wall. The forest grows luxuriantly along the heights, small mountain brooks come gushing down, or water oozes from moss-grown stones and drips down on flowering knolls of plants I did not know. Then the valley widens out. In the rice fields delicate green tufts, the young plants, stood in water which mirrored the blue summer sky. At the edge of the dark forests bamboo brakes arched, so golden and graceful that it was an everlasting joy to look at them. And the villages – how the Japanese peasants live I do not know, presumably not too well. But nothing could be more beautiful than their houses, with the pointed gables of their straw roofs, and walls of unpainted wood shimmering like silk. Now and then we went past a small temple; the entrance gate, the *torii,* has the same beautiful lines throughout. And behind them lie the small gray buildings, gray stone lanterns, gray stone lions flecked with golden lichen, in a grove of dark old trees. Nature and refined landscape art have combined to create beauty and restful harmony at even the smallest and poorest sanctuaries.

In Maibara we separated from those of our traveling companions who were going to Tokyo. Maibara lies on the shore of a large lake, Biwa; on the other side run high mountain chains, one behind another, losing themselves in the sunny haze and summer skies. But now the cities began to get larger, thickly populated districts set in.

Beginning a good distance above Osaka and continuing all the way down to Kobe are towns and villages nearly grown together into one city. I could not help thinking what an easy task it would be to bomb to bits all these immense stretches of closely packed, small, light wooden houses and burn up the whole affair. There are endless city sections with only such small wooden houses, even in cities with a nucleus of modern brick and concrete buildings and great factories, like Osaka and Kobe.

2

At the hotel in Kobe we received the first news from Europe since we had left Stockholm. It was not exactly encouraging. France, disarmed and humbled, Estonia, Latvia, and Lithuania swallowed up by Soviet Russia – England still unconquered, but now long would it last before the English also would be forced to lay down their arms?

And still at times we almost forgot it, at times I was so happy that I myself did not understand how I could be. The first evening we had gone down in the city and wandered at random in and out of the narrow, cramped streets. The open shops were full of varied wares that overflowed out on the sidewalk and almost obstructed people's way. Electric lights and colored lanterns and subdued golden lights behind the paper windows in the upper stories of the houses flowed together below, and high above us we sensed the velvet dark of night, which made the city snug and homelike. The night was sultry, full of strange and alien smells, but through it all we recognized the fragrance of oleander in bloom and the ocean air.

Seen more closely, most of what they had to sell in the shops was poor and cheap. The fruit-dealers had placed the best peaches and the ripest watermelons on top; underneath was unripe and speckled fruit – but heavens, they do that in other places in the world too. The vegetables looked withered – but they might have been fresh that morning. Small eating-places displayed beautiful porcelain bowls of food which looked extremely delicious; it looked better than it tasted, we discovered, when we went into a place to try a Japanese evening snack. But never mind – the food at the hotel was all right.

There was a whole quarter of dry-goods stores, with mostly European clothes, and poor and ugly they were, but ridiculously cheap. We hunted high and low, to see if it were possible to find some shirts for Hans; after the trip through Russia he was almost destitute of clothes. We found only a single one which he could use, although it also was too short in the sleeves. The Japanese do not look so small, but when one tries to find ready-made clothes and shoes one discovers how much taller and larger-limbed we Europeans are.

Toriis, old and gray, spanned the streets in many places. And in the midst of the confusion of shops and small houses was a small Shinto temple, with all its accompaniment of stone lions, stone lanterns, barriers, and God knows what. Under the old pine tree which shaded the temple entrance, there was, on the other side of the street, a shooting gallery; a gigantic oleander bush in bloom spread its branches over both the temple roof and a small shop which sold mineral water. – The whole bazaar quarter was evidently built on land which had originally belonged to the temple.

It seems impossible for foreigners to be able to learn anything definite – or come to a real understanding – of the Japanese people's religious life. Some people assure one that everything consists in observing certain ceremonial usages and reciting prescribed prayer formulas. Others explain it in this way: that it is the whole Japanese concept of existence that is so fundamentally religious that we Europeans can no longer understand it. We have in reality all become hard-boiled materialists; the belief in a spiritual reality back of the phenomenal world is reduced to, at the most, a conjecture or a vague hope. To the Japanese the phenomena, the fatherland, the imperial house, the dead and unborn representatives of the family, the changing seasons, and every feature in the life of the landscape and vegetation are only expressions of an immaterial reality. Even gods and spirits and the souls of the dead are worshipped as concrete forms of a reality on whose ruling powers man is dependent but which he never will be able to comprehend fully. Still others assert that at one time this was true; but now the official religion is only a part of the mechanism by which the ruling faction – themselves agnostics – maintain their absolute power over the people, who year by year are required to make greater sacrifices and are placed under new restrictions, to the advantage of this party's politics and greed. – A Norwegian lady who had lived in Japan for more than twenty years declared that the common Japanese people are very pious and live up to their faith in a way from which we could learn much. The son of her old housekeeper had recently become a

Buddhist priest, and she only wished all Norwegian divines lived such exemplary lives and served their Church and their fellow men with the unselfishness and self-sacrifice of this young Japanese priest.

That the Japanese should be irreligious by nature, as many insist, seems improbable, when one thinks, for example, of the history of the Catholic Church in Japan. During the persecutions in the seventeenth century, Japanese Catholics by thousands met torture and death with unequaled courage. And afterward the descendants of these martyrs held fast to their forbidden religion, deprived of priests, deprived of the sacraments, without any kind of buildings for the exercise of their faith, through more than two centuries. So when the old edicts which forbade Christian worship were rescinded in 1873, it appeared that there were still more than two thousand Japanese Catholics in Nagasaki and the near-by provinces. – Had I suspected that our stay in Japan was to be as long as it was, I would have taken Hans with me on a pilgrimage to the martyr hill and cathedral at Nagasaki.

One thing is certain, that at all the temples I saw in Japan men, and sometimes women, came and went in a steady stream. At the Shinto sanctuaries they perform a kind of devotions which, as far as I could see, follow this procedure: Those who pray pull a bell rope, to call the attention of the gods or spirits. Then they slip some coins in a box before the barrier which sets apart the inner sanctuary – a kind of altar with various sacred objects, the meaning of which I do not know, but which looked beautiful. Now the worshipper claps his hands, says a prayer (I suppose that is what it is), and performs a number of ceremonial bows before he withdraws. – At the little temple in the bazaar quarter in Kobe people came and "rang" all day long.

Many Shinto temples are dedicated to the memory of the dead – the spirits of men who in their earthly existence have in some way made themselves worthy to be honored by the people. General Nogi's former home in Kyoto, for example, is now arranged as a temple for the worship of his spirit. And in the outskirts of Kobe there is a large group of temples, where Kusunogi-Massashige is worshipped as the pattern of Japanese love of country, loyalty to the Emperor, and bravery; it was on the shore here that he lost the battle against the revolutionary army under the traitor Nitta-Yoshisada and finally committed hara-kiri in the year 1337. In the park surrounding the sanctuary is a row of trophies from Japan's most recent wars: Russian cannon from Port Arthur, parts of a Russian plane; whether any of the trophies date from the present war with China I do not know. But no doubt the war is the reason why this temple is visited just now by so many young men who go from chapel to chapel and hold devotions. Before the altars fluttered great numbers of small streamers and papers covered with writing, and thin sheets of wood on which the picture of a stallion had been burned. The other side of these sheets is arranged so they can be sent as postal cards from the temple. The surrounding park was beautiful, with large, dark pine trees and long avenues of stone lanterns and animal sculptures – lions, turtles, horses. Young ladies with small children walked in the avenues, rested and drank lemonade at the many small shops near the entrances, bought souvenirs. The Japanese seem to regard temple visits as pleasure trips, in which worship alternates with rest under the trees, and the aesthetic impressions from beautiful buildings and tasteful grounds are a part of the edification.

3

The newspapers told of arrests of aliens and an unmistakable trend toward a growing hostility to foreigners – at any rate, all foreigners who spoke English. As a commentary on the revolting stories about Japan's brutal treatment of the population in the occupied parts of China, the Europeans who had lived in Japan for years could tell of corresponding brutalization of life there. The people themselves are said to be so afraid of the police and its methods now that it is quite common for a thief, for example, to kill himself when there is danger of his being arrested; one of our acquaintances mentioned casually that recently there had been a burglary in her summer villa up in the mountains, but though she knew very well who was guilty, she had not the heart to report him. Both prostitutes and the geishas, heroines of many romances, are now often treated by the Japanese patrons themselves in a way which formerly only drunken sailors from European boats would allow themselves. And it was most earnestly enjoined upon us that if we wanted to take the trip along the coast toward Akashi, we must behave with the utmost care – for God's sake, not take pictures or show interest in places not pointed out by the guide; the coast, the bay, and the islands in the bay are military territory, and all foreigners who travel there are kept under sharp observation at all times.

Still, to begin with, it was difficult to make oneself believe that Japan was a country at war. The first impression was that here life went on swimmingly; people were well dressed, looked well fed and contented. They stopped in the streets in groups which conversed, merry and smiling, and separated after many bows and compliments. There were a number of beggars, but not nearly so many as, for example, in Moscow. In the side streets women sat on the balconies and sewed; newly washed clothes hung on lines at each house, crowds of children played in the streets. Often I saw in the temple parks groups of older girls or boys who sat peacefully with books or painting materials, read and sketched. The clerks in the shops were extremely obliging, willingly brought out almost the whole stock, but did not try to persuade us to buy. The personnel at the stations and our fellow travelers on the trains were all ready to do us a service, and offered explanations and help often before we asked them.

If, like me, one has at some time in one's youth allowed oneself to be quite bewitched by Lafcadio Hearn's Japanese sketches, one gives up unwillingly the idea that something must still remain of a beauty so marvelously harmonious, so beauty-filled, refined, and highly elaborate a culture as that of Japan – in spite of industrializing, Europeanizing, militarism of the German pattern. Grant that it was said, even at the time when Hearn wrote his descriptions, that he idealized, that Japanese reality had never been nearly so poetic as he made it. The country's fairyland beauty, the innumerable evidences of a highly developed artistic culture, as one finds it in the architecture, in a landscape art and horticulture which stand heaven-high above anything corresponding to them in the West, in all products of Japanese art and crafts – all this supports one's old predilection: one wishes to believe it is a clique that has seized for itself all the power in the country, the oppressed and eradicated democratic forces in the nation's political life were more genuine expressions of the people's nature. The responsibility for Japanese crimes against the neighboring peoples – "Nippism" I heard a Chinese call this Eastern variety of totalitarian-state brutality – rests wholly on one party in the country; the people themselves are as much the victims of this party as they are its fellow criminals.

"We smile and smile, but our hearts weep," the Norwegian lady who had lived in Japan for years quoted a Japanese friend who had just received from China the fifth little white casket with the ashes of one of her nearest relatives. Two sons, a brother, and two nephews had fallen there; she still had her husband and her only living son at the front. – Two or three times we met soldiers' funerals in the streets: a bus full of officers, each with a small white casket of ashes, carried in a kind of white shoulder scarf, and beyond the officers women dressed in mourning.

Still, Japan's losses in the war with China are small compared, for example, with the lists of the fallen during the former World War in Europe or the losses in this war during each of the German thrusts. And it has always taken long to break a people's will for war if it believes its existence is threatened. Will for war does not have much to do with enthusiasm for war – one is the instinct for self-preservation, the other most frequently an artificial product. It is probable that large portions of the people stand behind the originators of Japan's conquest politics. The dream of becoming lords over as many as possible of the Pacific countries and gaining power to utilize their natural resources for the benefit of the Japanese is undoubtedly extremely tempting for the masses in a country which is densely populated, by nature not very richly provided with anything but beauty; and the old social conditions, from the time when the Japanese people were easily satisfied in everything except their demands for perfect ethical and aesthetic modes of life – to them no way is likely to lead back.

That the state of war from the present must impose on the people privations and restrictions of many kinds will hardly make any particular impression on that section of the people which places its hope in the future, when the conquests will have been carried through and consolidated. Some of the sacrifices called for were almost funny – for example, the appeals to patriotic women, who were exhorted to renounce haircuts and permanent waves and go back to genuine Japanese styles of hairdress. The old-fashioned complicated masterpieces of the hairdressing art I did not see (but they are said to be in use still in festival occasions). Now most Japanese ladies wear their hair very simply, but gracefully and becomingly – parted in the middle and brushed back in soft, loose waves, into a knot at the nape of the neck. Short hair or "long bobs" and American kinds of permanents were as a rule extremely unbecoming. On the whole, though the Japanese women dressed with beauty and exquisite taste as long as they were in Japanese costume, their dress was clumsy and dowdy to an equal degree when they followed European fashions, and they certainly showed no noteworthy taste in choice of colors or cut. What there was of European furniture, pictures, and trinkets displayed in the shops was also quite ghastly. It was not only the busts of Hitler that betrayed their German origin; most of the Western articles which were for sale were obviously German trash, cheap and hideous. But this fallibility of taste in regard to products of an alien culture is certainly not one-sided. I am certain that a great many of the Japanese *objets d'art* which tourists buy in quantities (because they are so cheap, you know) are manufactured exclusively with the tourist trade in mind; no Japanese of the lower middle classes or his wife would have anything of the kind in the house. The "grand" Japanese kimonos of shiny silk covered with embroidery, immense dragons in gold threat, or wistaria vines, peonies, plum branches, and the like, in great coarse stitches and gaudy colors, I suspected no Japanese woman could be made to put on for love or money. I asked the clerk in one of the larger silk businesses at Monomati, the best shopping street, about this. The man laughed a little; then he brought out from another part of the shop the most beautiful cotton kimonos, in subdued colors and restrained patterns, plain-colored silk kimonos decorated with a simple, small notif, the Fujiwara – or Tukugawa – escutcheon: "If you wish something of the kind we like ourselves – but foreigners usually prefer what looks like more for the money."

I had gone into this shop to buy material, natural-colored shantung, for shirts and pajamas for Hans, summer dresses for myself. We had trudged through the city and ransacked Kobe's largest department store and various shops without being able to find anything in the way of ready-made clothes, which we needed badly now. So we had to have them made to order, and the street below our hotel was full of tailoring establishments. Meanwhile it was impossible to procure anything except artificial silk in all Kobe. The friendly, smiling clerk informed us that the entire Japanese output of natural silk goes abroad, for the manufacture of parachutes.

Along the whole street below the Tor Hotel, where we stayed, were shops which were entirely dependent on their sales to tourists from Europe and America. Now the trade here had decreased to a frightful degree. We were offered really excellent things in porcelain, lacquer, semi-precious stones, and enameled copper at ridiculously low prices. With a frankness that seems to be characteristic of Japanese merchants, it was pointed out that the newest lacquer ware was much inferior in quality to the older, of which there was still a little in stock; the technique of Japanese lacquer work really demands a mixture of gold leaf in the foundation colors – that is what gives it glow and sheen – and the painted decorations should be carried out in real gold. But now for more than a year it had been impossible to secure gold for this work.

This type of restriction can hardly work great hardships on the people in general. And it was especially European housewives who complained that for months at a time it had not been possible to get the least bit of white wheat flour; they were forced to serve soups and gravies unthickened, and could not bake cakes or biscuits. The hotels, however, still served rolls, and on the whole evidently had all they needed for use in the kitchen.

It was the threatened fuel shortage which made both foreigners and the Japanese themselves look forward to the winter with anxious forebodings. Even charcoal they were afraid would be scarce by winter. But that also is harder on the foreigners – the Japanese themselves are more resigned to freezing in the cold season.

What was really alarming was that even now there was a scarcity of rice, the most important food-stuff of the people. We were told: "Whatever you do, do not eat rice dishes in the Japanese restaurants. For if the improbable should happen, that a patron does not scrape the bowl to the last kernel of rice, you may be sure that what is left will be kept and served in the next portion."

The rice harvest was said to look promising. But Japan cannot raise nearly enough rice for its own use. The working population has for the most part lived on imported rice – of inferior quality, and cheaper than the home-grown. To provide such rice in sufficient quantities Japan will now be forced to try to extort the crops from the back provinces of India – on terms which Japan itself will dictate.

So in Japan also little by little we got the feeling that here too the living-conditions of the populace were subject to the same law which seems to operate in all totalitarian states: the standard of living sinks surely and steadily (even though in Japan it is still far above the depths to which it has sunk, for example, in Germany and Soviet Russia). But here too the people are required to submit to more and more restrictions, to the lack of satisfactions, large and small, which they had accustomed themselves to take for granted, and to give up more and more of their freedom to live and move according to their own wishes and inclinations. Even the newspapers which are published in English were full of patriotic harangues about this being the time to show heroism; now a less material spirit should be born, for the sake of a great and glorious future, when the nation would be able to roll in wealth. But when that future would come was not mentioned – and Heaven knows when it will come. And the only method which the rulers know of attaining the promised land for their people is to conquer neighboring countries and pillage neighboring peoples of everything of value they have achieved through hundreds of years of work.

4

The *S.S. President Cleveland* had been delayed once, twice. Day in and day out I was awakened by the strange, shrill, penetrating song of the cicadas, – some gigantic creatures who performed in a chorus of a hundred voices on the wooded mountainside toward which my hotel window opened. On the steep paths through the trees small Japanese boys with lime twigs would climb, catch the cicadas, and put them in tiny cages of sticks and straw; they keep these insects as we keep canaries and think the grating noise they produce is beautiful. And in fact I thought so too when I had accustomed myself to it. The music of the cicadas and the sound of clattering wooden slippers over flagstones will probably be what I shall think of as expressing the essence of Japan.

It was melting hot. Violent thunderstorms and pouring rains some afternoons cooled the air for only an hour or two; then the humidity made it seem even more suffocatingly warm. And I had a great deal to run about the town and attend to. Down to the office of the President Line, out to try on dresses – And then there was this traveling companion of ours from Prague who had been detained in Tsuruga, we had to try to do something for him. With Mr. G. I visited consulates and offices for refugee aid.

The young Jewish woman who was at the head of such an organization – she was herself a refugee from Germany – came to the hotel one day to have tea with me. She was entirely worn out from overwork and from all the misery which she had witnessed through what would soon be many years. One of the groups she had just recently succeeded in placing at the hospice they operated had come from Poland – some forty men who had been confined in a concentration camp. At last they had been told that they would be set free, given permission to leave. Then some of the German guards came: "Certainly not, – never imagine you will be allowed to go to Russia, no, now, you are going to be executed, and in a way that serves you right." They were driven to a crematorium and locked in the oven. The guards explained that now they would turn on the electricity. Harassed and shattered by all they had experienced, the men thought they could feel the room get hotter and hotter. Two died of heart failure, several others went entirely to pieces, were wrecks, when they were let out again after two hours had passed. It had just been a joke, the prison guards explained, laughing. So they were allowed to go. At any rate, this was the story as one of these newcomers told it to her. He was a man in his twenties; his hair was completely white.

So when the man from Prague one fine morning walked into the dining-room of the hotel, just as we sat at breakfast, we nearly pulled his arms out of their sockets, we were so glad to see him again. But Shanghai was the only place to which he could go, and the funds which by our joint efforts we had managed to scrape together for him would undeniably not go far in meeting expenses there for an indefinite time. Nor were there great prospects of his getting work there, I suppose – at least not as an artist in ceramics. But at any rate it was better than nothing.

Meanwhile it became evident that Hans and I would at least have time to go to Nara for a day, and take a two-day trip to Kyoto.

The city of Nara proper lies at the foot of a low, wooded mountain range, but beyond the city extends a large plain, framed by chains of mountains which are stretched into longer waves, not split in sharp peaks like the mountains in Tsuruga and the Rokko Mountains back of Kobe. With our limited time it was out of the question to see much of the city itself, for I wanted to see at least Horyuji, one of the oldest Buddhist monasteries in the country, with collections of old Japanese art, sculpture and paintings, which I had been familiar with through pictures for years, and never dreamed I should have a chance to see.

We drove by automobile through fields of garden-stuff, rice fields where a little water still stood between the light-green plants. Along the high mounds of grassy turf which separated the cultivated fields were planted rows of a kind of tall bean which now was flowering in large, fragrant, violet-red clusters; I suddenly realized why the most charming of all the heroines in an old Japanese romance is called Lady Beanflower. – Japanese peasants lead a life of drudgery and are, I think, wretchedly poor; barelegged, knock-kneed, burned dark brown by the sun, with the same deeply wrinkled necks that farmers get the world over, they waded between the rice plants, bent under large yellow straw hats shaped like mushrooms. But even these poorest people in Japan have their share in the country's most marvelous treasure – a sense of beauty so remarkably refined that we in Europe have nothing comparable. Every small house in the villages through which we passed was beautiful – many, sheer masterpieces in the graceful lines of their arched straw roofs, with walls of unpainted panels gleaming like silk – set between trees which skilled hands had clipped and bent to bring out the characteristic quality of each kind, so they looked more natural than nature. In the small villages the temples were separated from the roads by a water-filled ditch in which the tall-stemmed giant leaves of the lotus pushed one another upward; some last yellow-white flower saucers still lifted themselves between the throng of leaves and the beautiful urn-shaped seed pods.

Horyuji, beyond the monumental temple door, was a fairy-tale in a world apart. I do not know what it is now, but once it must have been a place where human beings who longed to discover a spiritual world of beauty behind the shifting forms of the material and the storms of passion could attain to a vision of eternity. In the shadow of ancient cedar trees and cryptomeria stretched long, low temple buildings, their woodwork gray-brown with age and golden patterns of lichen on the gray-blue, glazed tile roofs; pagodas and pavilions rose out of feather-light golden bamboo brakes. The first raindrops of a storm which was brewing lured forth a fragrance of earth and strange flowers and a good homelike smell of pine trees.

A number of the art treasures which are

preserved in Horyuji are shown to visitors only on certain days of the year. But what we were able to see was wonderful enough. The influence of Indian art is unmistakable in some of the oldest things, but statues and pictures get more and more beautiful the more the Japanese free themselves from it and find their distinctive quality. – A little white-haired sacristan, with a delicate, narrow face and clear eyes, brown as marsh water, led us through the groups of temple buildings. I do not know whether it was only Japanese politeness, or whether the old man really thought it was pleasant to have a listener who was so eager to learn something of his religion, but in his broken English he tried with all his might to explain to Hans what a Buddha is, and who they were, all these different Buddhas, what they meant, the strange Indian demons and idols, sages and hermits and hovering angels. Hans asked and probed, and the more he asked, the more smiling and friendly the old man became; he tried to make clear to Hans, the purpose of all these long recitations and prayer services which were going on around us in different chapels. My questions he almost wholly disregarded, with polite smiles and shakes of the head. So I did as the Japanese women do: followed the male head of my family at a respectful distance and in silence.

The park at Nara – according to the guide-book, the most beautiful in this country of beautiful parks – we saw as a dream vision, under a heavy veil of rain. We had to get out of the car, of course, to look at the famous deer which are found here by the thousands, and butt their visitors if they do not think they get enough tidbits – and we were drenched. Then into the car again and on, past temples which the dusk was already beginning to draw into the depths of the forest, past gray-green fields where a frieze of light-brown deer grazed along the wall of black cryptomeria and pine trees, over arched bridges with gushing brooks underneath. And back to the station in the town. Afterward you think this must be something you have dreamed – and wish you might be allowed to dream it again.

In Norway we have always been proud of our old art of building in wood. For at least a thousand years – from viking times until far on into the nineteenth century – we have built ships, houses, churches, from the timber in our forests. The long and intimate acquaintance with the natural quality of the material and all its possibilities had gradually developed a technical mastery of this craft which is unequaled in all Europe. Familiarity with the medium led to that certainty of taste which characterized our viking ships, our fishing boats, our old wooden churches, and our farm homes. It amused me to see in Japan, in some of the oldest buildings I saw there, that the structural problems had been solved in a way surprisingly similar to what was done in Norway – or, rather, it was natural that there was such a similarity. But the development in Japan has led to more rich and varied forms. The climate has surely had a good deal to do with this. It has made it possible for Japanese architects to develop the structural joints of the woodwork into decorative parts of the buildings; in Norway the people's desire to carve and color was driven within doors. And in Japan the house and garden have for more than a thousand years been conceived as a unit; open verandas and thin panel walls which can be pushed aside make the house and garden blend into one throughout the whole long summer. In Norway the cultivation of gardens is relatively new. Except for a period in the Middle Ages, when some large estates and small cities, following the example of the monasteries, laid out gardens, it was not until the eighteenth century that interest in gardening began to awaken in Norway. – Another thing which led the development of Japanese architecture into new ways and brought variety into its forms was the impulses from China and India which came with Buddhism. The pagodas are peculiar to the Buddhist temples; the Shinto sanctuaries are consistently built in simpler styles than the Buddhist.

Sanjusangendo in Kyoto, built in 1252, affected us both as something new and something with which we had long been familiar. An oblong four-cornered hall, with the roof resting on several rows of massive pillars. Our kingly halls from the same time must, according to the descriptions in the sagas, have looked something like this. It is in Sanjusangendo that there are a thousand and one statues of Kwannon, the goddess of mercy.

The effect was strangely moving. Mild and subdued, the daylight streams into the large hall, and against the old red-brown timber of the walls and roof and rows of pillars stands this host of slim, golden figures, the same, repeated a thousand times, arranged in five rows, each row raised a step higher than the row in front. The figure is strongly stylized and expresses immovable and tender tranquility. In the middle is enthroned a large sitting figure – Kwannon on Buddha's lotus throne, or Buddha himself, I do not know; the Japanese impersonation of eternal mercy is sexless. But not in such a way that anything seems to be lacking in these strange exalted beings; they give the impression of an abundant unity in which the nature of man and the nature of woman have not yet been separated. Hans assured me, however, that Kwannon is Buddha, and Buddha is Kwannon – and Kwannon-Buddha and all bodhisattvas are only changing forms of a unity which also is present hidden in each and every one of us. After his long conversation with the sacristan in Horyuji he was inclined to express himself authoritatively about Buddhism.

The impressions one receives from the places of worship of a religion one does not know much about are probably quite mistaken, or, rather, they undoubtedly are. A casual visitor imagines that what he sees means something quite different from what it means to the believers. But this dark hall with its throng of dull gold statues which are all images of a godlike mercy affected me at least quite powerfully, as an expression of something elemental in all religions which have attained to the idea that between the divine and the human there is a gaping abyss. How it is possible to bridge this abyss – if we, with ever so great and daring efforts can build bridges with our own power, or if God Himself must be the bridge-builder – that is the center of the fundamental disagreements between the great religions. But no Christian – at any rate, no Catholic Christian – should deny the heroic will toward such a bridge-building from our side of the gulf; and so one does not leave Sanjusangendo without being intensely and deeply moved. The eternal and unchangeable heavenly mercy, as it is expressed in this multitude of Kwannon figures, is not like our mercy – a feeling which rises like an ocean wave, only to fall back again and lay bare the wreckage of slime and hate and cruelty. It is eternal, unchangeable, not mortal – and therefore to us it may seem inhuman – but he who has once attained to a little glimpse of what Buddhists call Kwannon knows that in spite of all, there is no true worth in our mercy except as it reflects Kwannon, the heavenly mercy.

The other temples in Kyoto which we were able to see in two days – in a city in which one could certainly live for months without gaining more than a quite superficial acquaintance with the treasures of beauty and art it contains – gave me, at any rate, no religious impression, either true or mistaken. They were fascinating, as Italian Renaissance villas or old English manors are – the same thing in a different way. Surrounded by parks, which without noticeable transition lose themselves in the mountain woods, lie temples which are pearls of Japanese architecture. Some as refinedly simple, airy, and light as the "golden pavilion" at the edge of a little pond with green water and artificial islets out in the pond. Under the bridge which leads out to the pavilion swift goldfish flash and sluggish turtles crowd in heaps and drowse between iris and rushes at the water's edge. Others seem monumentally impressive, like Kiyumizu. The chief temple is built on a skillfully constructed platform over a crevice in the mountain. But at each turn of the road in the park, along the banks of the mountain stream and at the graceful forest lakes, one comes upon the most beautiful small temples and pagodas which lie scattered between bamboo brakes and maple groves and groups of pine trees.

The community museum in Kyoto is modern, spacious, and admirably arranged. And it houses a splendid collection of Japanese art and crafts – strongly stylized sacred sculpture and realistic sculptures of renowned teachers and sages of ancient times, fantastically lifelike pictures of ugly and beautiful and strongly individualized old men. And one goes through room after room full of paintings from many times and style periods.

Kyoto and the surrounding country are the setting of Lady Murasaki's heroic romance about Prince Genji's almost innumerable love-affairs. The book was written some time between the years 1000 and 1020, but the action is set some generations earlier. It was at the time when Europe was working its way out of the chaos of the "Dark Ages" – in Norway the viking age had just ended. But in so far as the milieu of Murasaki's romance suggests any period in Europe's history, it is the eighteenth century. In reality, it is very reminiscent of *l'ancien régime* in France, or of the "Gustavian period" in Sweden. Genji himself is not at all unlike, for example, Gustavus III's famous favorite, Gustaf Mauritz Armfelt, without Armfelt's military and political energy; although the authoress informs us that Genji is occupied with state affairs – which he as much as possible leaves to others, and which Murasaki moreover does not feel herself qualified to depict, since she is a woman. But he seems to do little besides worship nature, art, and ladies, and act as connoisseur of all phases of the ancient Japanese art of living. Like Armfelt, Genji has a wife whom he loves above all other women – which does not prevent him, any more than it prevented Armfelt, from feeling that he must win every woman who awakens his slightest interest. Even the kind of love which Murasaki pictures, in innumerable variants and degrees of intensity, is very like the eroticism of the *fêtes galantes* in Europe. They are the same kind of adventures, brought about by curiosity, or because it would be a pity to let a piquant situation go to waste, but then they very often develop into serious affairs of the heart, which heroes and heroines foster with torrents of tears, through bitter complications, and by assiduous searchings of their own and their partners' emotions. Murasaki's accounts of all these lovers' shifting feelings are amazingly acute and full of subtle observations. In European literature it was still to be hundreds of years before the interest in such psychological miniature-painting awoke. On us, therefore, Murasaki makes an unbelievably modern impression. In reality the type of erotic she describes is timeless (even if it is not manifest everywhere and at all times) and universal: it is love life as it flourishes within a class of society where nobody needs to work for his living or his social position.

It is a good thing for young ladies to be beautiful, but still better to be of noble family; best, of course, to be related to the imperial house. This does not prevent their being deeply and romantically unhappy, but it at least raises them above the broad mass of the people, whom Murasaki does not even consciously despise – they hardly exist for her, the life they live is something different from what she means by life. No woman can be attractive unless she has had a meticulous upbringing: she must be intellectual (that is, she must be able to converse, quote or improvise verses appropriate to every occasion), play one or more musical instruments with taste and skill, and be able to compose and write beautiful and elegant letters. At Murasaki's imperial court nobody, not even servants, men or women, of the lowest classes, is illiterate – something which is undeniably impressive when one thinks of what a comprehensive discipline Japanese writing is.

The complex system of ranks and the elaborate etiquette which creates so many complicated problems, the innocent inevitability with which those in the capital look down upon the residents of the provinces and people from the country – even for a lady who has been elevated to the rank of Empress, it is painful to remember that she was born in Akhashi – it all impresses one as very rococo. One reads the long romance at first captivated and charmed by the enchanting nature descriptions and by Murasaki's gracious and complete unveiling of all things human within a certain social frame. And then gradually one grows a little weary – quite weary at last. And when one has finished the romance of Genji one is heartily glad that period is past, both in Europe and in Asia. Nobody knows how the world will look when this war is ended – I, at any rate, am afraid it will be long, perhaps several generations, before the world has overcome its aftermaths. But at least it is well, I think, that the taste for the aristocratic idyll is dead. For the time being, at least.

In Japan the Middle Ages followed the rococo – the iron age, and age of chivalry, civil war between the chieftains of the great noble houses, after the time of the *fêtes galantes*. Japan's Middle Ages, when the Emperior's power became a mere shadow, and the whole people suffered each time one of the barons, the chieftains of the clans, did his best to exterminate his rivals, whole noble families, with women and children and all their followers, fall in the same period as the barons' wars in Europe and in many ways resemble Europe's Middle Ages. Here as there art and learning had their periods of flowering in spite of the violent convulsions within society, here as there it was a time of religious passion and religious unrest. Japan's age of chivalry ended when Hideyoshi, a peasant boy and an officer in the army of a murdered feudal chief, avenged his lord, crushed a series of the mightiest clans, and let the Emperor name him regent of the country.

That was the beginning of the Shogun dynasty. And while the Shoguns ruled in Edo, and the Emperior sat in Kyoto, as a powerless slave of his incomprehensible holiness, Japan became a closed country in which no strangers were permitted to set foot. Isolated from the outer world, they could again devote themselves completely to the development of a highly elaborate culture, national, ethical, and aesthetic, with an intricately contrived system of etiquette for all life's situations and conditions, and a rigorous division of people into classes. The poorest were very poor, but they also had their share in the inheritance of beauty, their place in the year's procession of flower festivals, and festivals for the gods and the spirits of the dead, and festivals for the life and play of children. Until Commodore Perry in 1853 came and broke open the doors to the closed country. What the ultimate consequences of that achievement will be nobody knows.

We, the people in the countries which together have been the creators and bearers of Europe's civilization, had gradually come to regard it as self-evident that directions and tendencies which we believed we could trace through the entire development of this civilization – and which actually are found there – these were expressions of a law of nature. By this law all cultural development proceeded according to a set pattern, slower or faster in people of different civilizations. Tribes and races in which such a cultural development could not be shown we called primitive or backward people, and we never doubted our right to make ourselves their masters, to develop and educate them – on the condition that we could get compensation out of their countries and labor. Consciously and unconsciously we assumed that the history of the world was first and foremost the history of the triumphs of the white race. The goal of "progress" to this day has been to develop the European man and his descendant, the white man in America. And up to the day of the outbreak of the former World War most people had an absolute, optimistic confidence that this progress would automatically produce a continually better and wiser people, and happier, healthier living-conditions for all people. The English official or soldier who tried to bring Great Britain's colored subjects into his own type of civilization, the German Tiedemann, *entzückt* by the Hohenzollern kingdom's thoroughgoing order and discipline, the American citizen who never doubted that he lived in freedom's promised land and knew certainly that here science had been most completely tamed to play its new role as the handmaiden of money power, the Scandinavian schoolmaster who smilingly surveyed entire nations where every child received an education the worth of which it was heresy to question – every one could rejoice in the secret conviction that his people and his race were the very topmost twig on mankind's genealogical tree. Popular Darwinism has played a large role in the forming of this world picture. Gradually, as Darwin's ideas about the origin of species and the survival of the fittest, from being a working hypothesis for scientists, sank down to being a makeshift religion for the moderately enlightened middle classes, they took for granted that as biological development had progressed from "lower" (less complex) to "higher" (more complex) organisms, so "progress" would also provide that all human relations, customs, and laws and social forms would automatically proceed from "lower" to "higher" levels. And the highest forms were those which we ourselves and our nearest forefathers had helped to create. – But the background for this optimism regarding evolution was the Christian past of the white race. Pre-Christian pagans – Greeks and Romans and Nordic peoples, or redskins and Asiatic tribes – have usually conceived of the Golden Age as having been some time in the past. The present was hard, and the future was dark and full of menace. When the Christian Church began to speak and taught that God's kingdom would come, it was in reality challenging people's innermost convictions. The Church has, to be sure, never undertaken to prophesy when God's kingdom will be established on earth. And it has diligently reminded us that we both can do and are doing a great deal to delay its coming.

There were many things in the evolutionary teachings which popular Darwinism overlooked – or never had grasped. For example, that biological evolution, however else it has proceeded, has at least proceeded without any evidence of conscious or voluntary co-operation on the part of the organisms that evolved. When our grandparents and parents imagined that they saw evolution parallel to biological evolution in the development of conditions in large and small human communities – where prejudices against the new and the need for renewal, love of old familiar surroundings and revolt against them, fear and hope and hate and love and greed for power had always been shaping factors – then they yielded unconsciously to the poetic instinct in man's souls, which always tries to depict its experiences in figurative language and parables. When Linné in *The Marriage of Plants* recounted his observations as scientific investigator of sexual propagation in flowers, the poet in him asserted his rights; he describes his discoveries in an imagery in which rococo cupids flutter about his flowers like butterflies. There is, of course, this difference: that Linné knew what was observation and what was the play of his fancy. The adherents of evolution optimism did not recognize this difference, and that was fatal. Neither do they appear to have known that in the matter of capacity to withstand changes of environment, the ability to survive natural catastrophes, adapt themselves, and assure the continued existence of the species under changing conditions, the "highest," most complex organisms have not always been the most successful. The horseshoe crab is older on the earth than man, and it is certainly not improbable that it will survive us.

And still there is a solid kernel of truth in our parents' myths and legends, their belief that the peoples of Europe have developed their civilization through its entire historical period into something higher and nobler, and that when the immigrants from Europe brought their cultural inheritance with them to the newly discovered world across the Atlantic Ocean, much of what we had come to consider superior in it received new strength and vigor in the new soil, under new skies.

The determination to guarantee all people within

a social community a certain measure of rights and freedom is ancient among the western European peoples – even if nobody at the beginning of the historical period dreamed of guaranteeing all members of a community identical rights. The tendency was, at any rate – with backslidings and interruptions along the way – progress toward the creation of a greater equality, and increased freedom for all. The thought of the brotherhood of all men is Christian. We are all brothers, because we are all children of the same Creator God. We are all inheritors of the same bankrupt estate, since the first human pair sinned and squandered that glorious dowry which the Creator gave them when He created them. We are all fellow heirs to the glorious kingdom which Christ, our brother, won back for mankind. But far from all Christian people have drawn the same conclusions from this teaching of the brotherhood of man in God as the western European and the American: that in society here on earth brotherhood should lead to the same freedom and equality before the law, for all people. To many Christian people it seemed just as natural that the social status of brothers in Christ should be highly unequal as that brothers and sisters in the flesh should share unequally when a father's goods and privileges were inherited. So it was, for example, in Germany, and in many parts of Germany people have at times been intensely and fanatically pious Christians. It never saved the German peasants from being oppressed and held down in a poverty worse than in any other country. And they were not only looked down upon by the more privileged classes in the country – that was true over large parts of Europe, yes, finally even in the Scandinavian countries, where in the Middle Ages *bonde* ("farmer"; all Scandinavian peasants in the early Middle Ages were free men, yeomen or tenants; serfdom did not exist) had been a name of honor, so that a Norwegian King early in the 1100's could say in a poem that "to him *bönder* seemed the best." But the German peasant was abused, scorned, and reviled in a way so coarse that it makes much of the German literature of the Middle Ages unbelievably disgusting reading. And when the German peasants at the time of the Reformation rose in revolt against their oppressors, inspired by the religious unrest of the time, which made them read in the Bible the teaching about the equality of God's children even here on earth, then Martin Luther was the most high-voiced in preaching holy war against the peasants. He went so far in his zeal that he forgot as well his own teachings of the worthlessness of good deeds – promised the nobles that God would reward their work of strangling the peasant insurrection in peasant blood.

The ideas of the democracies about freedom, equality, and brotherhood are the fruits of Christianity in peoples which before they were Christianized had regarded freedom as the highest good in the world. It was here that the community of freeborn men, under the influence of Christianity, slowly spread out to embrace larger and larger strata of the populace, here there were steadily opened more and easier paths from the strata of men bound to serve into the ranks of independent men. The oldest Christian laws of Norway account the emancipation of slaves, the purchase of slaves to give them freedom on the year's greatest holidays, among the good deeds which people should practice to please Christ. The oldest Norwegian and Swedish and Danish laws, which all begin almost identically, "With law a country shall be built and not with lawlessness destroyed," remind us that law must be for all, it must not be made or written in favor of an individual; both rich and poor must let themselves be guided by the law. He who does not grant law to another, he himself shall not enjoy law.

It was the peoples along the coast of the Atlantic Ocean who, first and foremost, had this longing for freedom, this determination to make the community more spacious and build it on an increasingly reciprocal basis. – Just as the first experiments with democracy, with self-government by the citizens, were made by the seafaring Greeks, and the oldest republic in the Europe of today is Iceland, founded by seafaring Norwegian *bönder*, who would not submit to laws they themselves had not had a share in making.

Our fatal mistake has been that we, the nations around the North Atlantic, citizens of the ocean as much as of the dry land, have taken for granted that because we had found in democracy the way of life which made possible the realization of conscious and unconscious impulses existing in the souls of ocean-borne men, through thousands of years, so the longing of all races must have as its object freedom, equality, and brotherhood. And that they wished to arrive at a social form which offered the greatest possible, equality, freedom, brotherhood among nations, along the paths which we had always preferred. We too had sometimes been forced to carry on bloody battles to win this or that right, to gain increased freedom. But we always preferred to expand and improve our communities in peaceful co-operation between all our wisest men of the country, by discussing the problems which lay before us, finding our way forward by trial and experiment, determining matters vitally important to the country and the people in the assembly of the people. Experiments which intend to distill equalitarian societies by eradicating all variations from an arbitrarily conceived-of human type – in which the brain is transformed into a receiving apparatus for everything which the rulers decree, the thinking faculty of the individual is reduced to a kind of appendix without demonstrable function, like the vermiform appendix – are fundamentally alien to the peoples of the Atlantic Ocean countries. They have no links with any tendencies in our history.

That such experiments on the whole have been able to find advocates among the descendents of that European and American culture's founders is due to a crucial situation, which is not essentially different from crises we have gone through before, but which this time has a new form: Again we have reached a point where the fruits of our own ingenuity, our labors to increase our knowledge about the material world in which we live and to utilize our acquired knowledge to improve and make more secure our life on earth, have become so many and so manifold that we cannot cope with our own riches. Our knowledge and technique have become a horn of plenty; it pours out riches which rip apart old forms of society, and in the pangs and anxieties which this process brings upon the people, many forget that the very development of this new knowledge presupposes intellectual integrity, patience, co-operation, and free discussion of ideas between many fellow workers with widely different views of the problems. We should know, from the experience of some thousand years, that the effort to establish equality, brotherhood, and material happiness for a certain population type (still existing only as an imaginary figure) by liquidation of heterogeneous types and inconvenient kinds of capacities in nations – through murder, massacre, artificially produced famine, and mental poison – that is a "counsel of despair" which can never lead to anything except – something different from the intended goal. To accept one – or a second or a third – of the totalitarian state systems, to the people in the democratic states, would mean cutting off the branch on which they are sitting. The spiritual and material goods to which we had attained – which the totalitarian states envied us – in which the whole people everywhere were already sharing, even if an equal and just division of goods was still music of the future, these we had attained to by virtue of the democratic tendencies within the nations. The will to create states founded upon the idea of equity, with equal rights for all citizens, the determination to open a free path for every kind of ability regardless of the circumstances in which the individual was born and grew up, the respect for representative bodies and the faith that through free discussion between representatives of different opinions and points of view man would finally find the way to what was healthiest and best, would manage to sift facts from fancy and wishful thinking – these are the presuppositions for all that we hope to attain in a future which it is our earnest hope will give our children and grandchildren safer and happier conditions than our world has offered us. In other words, in the democratic nations we had arrived at the conviction that it must be possible to solve also the problems of man's social relations according to the same fundamental principles, which have made possible our conquests in the fields of science and technique. Of course, one cannot simply place the sign of equation between the so-called exact sciences and the social science, which must always operate with incalculable elements; no matter how much the sciences can discover about people, ultimately man will continue to be incalculable. But in so far as one can on the whole speak of scientific social building, the democracies are alone about it. The totalitarian-state systems build on fantasies and unscientific wishful dreams to such a degree that they are forced to chicanery even in the exact sciences for the sake of their wishful dreams. We have already heard of "Communistic science" and "Nazi science." But to believe that even, for example, technical or medical advances can build further on anything except pure science, honest science, is an illusion for which the totalitarian states will surely soon enough have to pay dearly.

The weaknesses of the democracies are easy to discover. When the entire people has the right to take part in the deliberations about ways and means for its future development, directly or indirectly, it is unavoidable that advances must come but slowly. The wagon must stop now and then, or roll backward on its upward journey. The road hog's ruthless driving toward future goals is not possible under democratic forms of government. A free path for all kinds of movements has all too often meant that men and women whose most eminent gift was the ability to elbow their way forward, or trample their fellow citizens underfoot, were allowed to do so unhampered – yes, were often admired by their victims, for undeniably they trampled forward on their cruel path with great talent. The evolution optimism has of course also led to an easy and highly unmotivated belief that man was essentially "benevolent." In the preceding century's fight against Christianity's "dogmas" the teaching about original sin was the first dogma which people tried to raze. No matter how merrily the seven deadly sins frolicked through society, the old ladies were given new and pleasant pet names, and good people hoped that if you would let them have more enlightenment and excuse them from education and repressions, provide increased material welfare and reduce your demands on devotion to duty, they would settle down and become good girls. To sift facts from fantasies and wishful thinking is easier said than done; for every hundred times we try it, we succeed in perhaps seven or nine cases. Which does not excuse us if we cease our strenuous effort and refuse to try a hundred times more.

For in spite of everything, with the world as it has become today, it is certain that the victory of democracy along the whole line is the only guarantee of a better future, for all nations and all peoples, through endless centuries. The new technique has brought all nations on our globe into connections so rapid and so unavoidable that there is no place where it is possible to escape from the forces for good and evil which the Western countries have set in motion. No longer can any people isolate itself from other peoples,

In spite of everything, there was some justification for the pride of the British administrator in the work he had achieved in the colonies on behalf of his country, to prevent the periods of famine which in many places cost ten thousand human lives each time the crop failed for one year, by the building of canals and communications. European doctors had a right to be proud of their fight against the bubonic plague, cholera, and leprosy, against sleeping sickness and hookworm. The German Biedermann was probably right when he believed that the Hohenzollern discipline and order ensured the greatest possible happiness for him and his kind – since the German masses were used to conceiving of law as a collection of orders and prohibitions, given them by a few men at the head of their society, and not as the expression of their own thoughts about justice and injustice, clothed in the words of representatives whom they themselves had chosen to make the law. Justice, for us Norwegians, for example, was a norm for our behavior in relation to other people, a norm which we had had a part in making; for the Germans, "justice" meant the laws and commands which tribunals and policemen saw to it were obeyed. And a people with such a mentality was certainly better off under the Hohenzollern rule than ever before – and probably better off than they will be again for an endless time. For even the Hohenzollerns were forced to give some slight consideration to the ideas about human values and human justice which had dominated the progress of their neighboring democratic states. The American had reason to be proud of the pledge for freedom which his vast country had redeemed time after time; he was right in his belief that in America more than in any other single country in the world science – besides helping the rich to get even richer – had helped every common man and woman who had not been completely defeated in the fight for a subsistence to added independence and improved living-conditions. Our Scandinavian schoolmasters had reason to be proud of their work to make a school education the right of every child in the country, if they had only not assumed so confidently that the state's taking charge of the whole educational system could not possibly be anything but a good and truly democratic arrangement. Never had they dreamed that this same system of instruction for which they had fought so bravely and enthusiastically would in the hands of a totalitarian-state leadership become the foremost instrument for burying whole generations of youth in ignorance and black superstition.

But all the same, and in spite of everything: Now the culture of the democracies must advance further along the lines it has followed for a thousand years, or succumb and carry with it into destruction all it has created and won for mankind. Civilizations have been able to develop to high stages quite differently, toward quite different ideals; for example, the way and ideal of Japan are exactly the reverse of ours. Certainly we can learn much from the culture peoples of Asia. We could learn much also from the cultures which we in schoolmasterly scorn of illiterates and materially poor civilizations have been used to call primitive. *But now all of these have learned a fatal thing from us.*

There is hardly any non-European people which does not have the right to accuse the white race of aggression, of stupid meddling in their way of living their lives, of exploitation. In their eyes it can hardly count as much as we think it should, that we, for example, have freed them from native diseases which had ravaged them from time immemorial, that we have forced them to give up folk customs which at least from our point of view meant perpetual suffering and terror for the weakest and most helpless – ritual cannibalism, slave-hunts, widow-burning – created new ways of life and taught them new ways of fighting drought, epidemics among their animals, natural catastrophes. Nor have we done it gratis; we have not done it for humanitarian reasons only, although it would be untrue to say that humanitarian grounds have not also often played a large role for us. All the same, there is no reason to expect that they will give us much thanks. But when people after people, in Asia and Africa, now stands up and protests against man's exploitation of man, demands self-government, demands freedom for its native country, then they surely have not sucked it from their own breasts. It is the encounter with the Western culture which has taught them the very word *Freedom*. It is the wine of the democracies which they have tasted and found pleasing.

That is not to say that they will use their self-government to rebuild their societies according to democratic principles. It is possible that they will use their national independence, once gained, to organize themselves internally as caste states, slave states, states where a small ruling caste, a racial minority in the country, or a few families rule unchecked over masses destitute of rights. It will mean an end of progress, as we conceive of progress. The peoples will set out on their forward march toward social conditions from which we have worked ourselves up hundreds of years ago, forward toward all which our nature led us to reject and change. This advance toward all which for us is out of date and intolerable is already in progress in many places on the earth, with bugles blowing.

So I knew even before Hans and I went on board the *President Cleveland*, which was to take us to San Francisco – let America be as different from Europe as it will, the United States has its own cultural forms, widely different from those of western Europe, of which it once was a scion. All the same, it was not only in body that we came nearer our own country each day the boat carried us over the Pacific Ocean, and the train took us from California to New York. After having fled from the Nazi invasion in Norway, through Soviet Russia and Japan, I knew that to come to America would still be to start the homeward journey. Now it is only across America that the road leads back to the future – that which we from the European democracies call future.

Return to the Future

Whenever I hear these hues and cries for Great Britain's peace aims, or the peace aims of the democracies, which people of "goodwill" constantly raise, I am reminded of a good old Norwegian adage: "Do not sell the hide before the bear has been shot."

Nevertheless, there are certain points of view and facts which it may be worth our while to note and examine. Of course, on the assumption that the democracies will finally succeed in hunting down the wild beast. Otherwise it will not be we who get anything to say when the future of the peoples is to be built up again. Instead it will be those who will drive mankind down into darkness. And we do not know if we, or our descendants, will have a part when man once more – perhaps only after centuries have elapsed – painfully begins to work his way into daylight again. I am fully convinced that the rulers of the totalitarian states cannot build any "new order." But nobody can know how thoroughly they will be able to destroy their victims if they can retain power over them long enough. Great culture-building peoples have before been practically eradicated from the surface of the earth. A small remnant of their descendants, reduced to fellahin or poor nomadic tribes, vegetate amid the ruins of their forefathers' cities and the memorials of a vanished, fine, and elaborately developed culture. We have no guarantees that we shall not meet such a fate. The war aims of the democracies must, to begin with, be the defense of their life, their existence as democracies. We hope, then, that we shall be able to accomplish this.

And after that we shall be forced to hunt our way back toward the future. It will not be easy. The work of clearing away the ruins, when this war has finally been fought to an end, will be enormous. It will mean to rebuild health in nations where millions of people have been destroyed by undernourishment and naked starvation, by hatred and by abnormal living-conditions, by inhuman and nerve-shattering experiences – where a generation of children has had the worst imaginable conditions in which to grow up during their formative years. It will mean to rebuild cities in ashes, rebuild a social and economic order on the ruins of an order which has collapsed during the war, to re-establish international trade relations, take up once more exchange of goods between countries whose production machinery has been smashed by the conquerors, to repatriate multitudes of people from the occupied countries who have been led away into slavery by the occupation powers – and all this in spite of the fact that after this war both the victors and the vanquished will be left with a depleted worn-out transportation system. It will be a gigantic task to try to re-create the moral defenses of faith, hope, and love which naked brutality and unparalleled injustice and a boundless hatred of the aggressors have burned to the ground. And last, but not least, if on the whole there is to be a prospect of a future for any people, then the courage and will to bear and foster a posterity will have to be re-established; but this is something we all know, that lax and irresponsible sexuality has always accompanied the state of war in all countries, and during this war it is surely excusable and understandable if young people in the democratic countries have arrived at the belief that the worst moral crime they can commit is to beget children, when one can do little to protect their childhood, nothing to assure their future – and the totalitarian enemies encourage brutal and shameless production of man-power to replenish their force of soldiers and executioners. It demands no less than heroic courage, of both men and women, to venture founding a new family in the midst of a war; and whatever security can be guaranteed families in the period immediately after the war will pretty certainly be of a dubious nature. Although it is a truth so obvious that it is embarrassing to mention it that the future of any society is determined by the life and prosperity of families within that society.

"When you call out in the forest, you get your own words back for an answer," says another Norwegian adage. (We Norwegians were always given to proverbs; in proverbs the experiences of our tribes and the wisdom of our fathers were

transmitted from generation to generation.) And
certain it is that if the people of Europe, within a
surveyable future, are to obtain livable
circumstances, and the opportunities for a fruitful,
creative co-operation, then we must in some way
prevent the echo of the vile infamies which Nazi
Germany has howled, roared, and shrieked out in all
the world's forests from being sent back toward a
conquered Germany from every forest and
woodland patch in Norway, Denmark, Poland,
Czechoslovakia, Austria, Italy, France, Holland,
Belgium, from the whole Balkan Peninsula, from
England and America. Hatred and thirst for revenge
are sterile passions. The most miserable poverty, the
most unthinkable filth and squalor, the
indescribable stench of refuse and decomposition
which I saw and smelled everywhere in Soviet
Russia are surely the fruit of the acceptance by
Russia's revolutionary heroes of a hate-consumed
old German Jewish writer named Karl Marx and
their identification of their future goals with his
dreams of revenge against everything that happened
to awaken his enmity.

The work of rebuilding a society of free nations
and free human beings, whose duty and right it is to
fight for a greater sense of responsibility between
man and man, for a higher justice, more secure and
happy living-conditions, will undeniably be
obstructed because the German people under
Hitler's leadership have managed to create a white-
hot hatred of Germany, of all things German, in all

countries and peoples outside Germany, and (perhaps?) in that small part of the German people which had accepted western European democratic ideas about culture and civilization, however alien these ideas are to the vast masses of the German people. But how in God's name will it be possible to neutralize that hate which consumes all the victims of Germany's lying and faithlessness, German sadism, German rapaciousness and greed, German grossness in the relations between the conqueror and the conquered – so that it does not completely paralyze all constructive forces in the peoples?

We Norwegians, settled for thousands of years in an unfruitful, harsh, long and narrow country, where the earth is locked by frost for more than half of the year, and our coast ravaged by storms, with tumultuous sea and blinding fog in the waters around our many thousands of islands and fjords for months at a time, we were always forced by the very nature of Norway to mobilize all there was in use of constructive forces. In reality, even the viking period, which to foreigners – naturally enough – seems to have been an era when the whole masculine portion of the Scandinavian population sailed in ships, plundered, murdered, and took from other nations their countries and their property, was at home such a constructive period. It was, in fact, by no means the whole people who roved as vikings, and the crews on the chieftains' viking ships were in large part farm boys who made some expeditions before they settled down in peace at home on their farms and worked the soil and the dairies. The art of obtaining the ore from our bogs, smelting and forging the marsh iron, was the economic basis of the viking expeditions; the newly discovered riches of native iron made it possible to build the ships, the finest watercraft of their time, and the manufacture of iron weapons on a scale than undreamed of. But the same newly discovered wealth of iron made possible also the clearing of whole districts which had before been primitive forest, better agricultural methods, the settlement of uninhabited or thinly populated islands and shores of the Atlantic Ocean. A comparison between the inventory list from royal estates in the Carolingian period in France and the burial gear which an old Norwegian farmer in moderate circumstances – owner perhaps of a horse, three cows, and a slave and a slave woman, plus some sheep and goats – of the same period had placed on his burial mound shows that the Norwegian farmer must have owned four or five times as much in iron tools and weapons as the establishment on the French kingly estate had at its disposal.

In the last century we had become fully convinced of how necessary it was for us Norwegians to *"löfte I flokk,"* "work together," if we as a nation were to achieve a life of security and moderate comfort in our difficult country. We had taught ourselves to guard the precious human lives, for there are only about three millions of us – about as many people as live in Brooklyn. We had become unwarlike, but we had certainly not become uncourageous. The kind of heroic exploits which we admired, however, were exploits of rescue. The captain who amid driving storm and snow sailed his little fishing boat straight over the submerged hull of a capsized companion boat, where drowning men clung to the keel, he was the hero among the Lofoten fishermen. While he let his boat fly over like a bird, his men lay stretched over the gunwale, pulled the capsized men out of the jaws of the ocean safe on board. Sometimes the captain had to make a return journey and sail over the boat several times before he had rescued all who would be rescued. The people in his home district told proudly how many lives such a daring and able captain had saved. It was our sailors we admired – the officers and crews on Norwegian ships who during the hurricane in the North Sea in 1938 labored days and nights to rescue the crews of the wrecked ships which drifted at the mercy of the storm, the young sailor who jumped in with a line tied around his waist and swam over to the wreck. We glowed with pride and happiness at being Norwegian, like these boys. Our pride was the little boy, the little schoolgirl, the young man, or the old woman who risked their lives to save a drowning fellow man out in the ice on a frozen sea, out in the rapids – and it was never long before we again had reason to rejoice over such a rescuing exploit. We were proud of the men who imperiled their lives to save some bodies so they could be honorably buried, when one of our commercial planes some years ago crashed against a shelf in one of the highest and most inaccessible mountain peaks on the west coast. To us the Germans come and say – after our little army of poorly trained, inadequately equipped soldiers, with the courage of lions, for sixty days had tried to defend our country against the invaders – that "we can win again our *Waffenehre*" (integrity, and honor in arms) "if Norwegians will enlist as German auxiliary troops."

The Germans' talk of Waffenehre has been called a medieval way of thought. It is true that *Waffenehre* is a medieval concept – but the Germans have forgotten, and they who call the present-day German way of thought medieval have, I dare say, never known that in the Middle Ages there was something which was called dishonoring one's arms. If in practice it was not always possible to destroy a strong and mighty scoundrel, in theory, at any rate, all were agreed that a man who misused his weapon in unjust and unclean causes deserved to have the beadle break his sword and crush his shield, tie the remnants to the tail of an ass, and let them be dragged in the mud.

In a report to the *New York Times* of March 29, 1941, David Anderson says: "It has been somewhat of a surprise for the British to see the intensity of the Norwegians' bitterness against the Germans. They are much more vindictive than the Dutch, French, Belgians, and Czechs." Can that surprise anyone? The others have tried injustice before, the others were not so unaccustomed to enduring invasion, to seeing the enemy perform low and cruel acts. The Norwegians have, day in and day out, for almost two years, seen foreigners enact crimes which we literally had ceased to believe any human being would make himself guilty of. Of course, we had read of how the Germans acted this way and that in Belgium, in Serbia, during the former World War. But we were more than willing to dismiss "atrocity stories" with a shrug of the shoulder – if they were not out and out lies, they were at least wildly exaggerated.

Children have been mistreated, women raped in Norway, too. But the criminals always proved to be human wreckage, imbeciles or defectives. We had become accustomed to believing that things like that were never the acts of normal people. I shall not tell "atrocity stories," but this I can say, that already enough horrors have happened in Norway to give our entire people a suspicion that in Germany today there are more abnormal than normal men. Men and women are imprisoned without legal grounds, prisoners tortured – we had forgotten such things could happen. Our system of justice is being broken down; and no people in Europe had so firmly rooted a respect for law and justice as we. Occasionally it degenerated into a mania for legal quibbling which was not without its comic sides. But at least for us law was not a collection of commands and prohibitions, enforced throughout the country by police and secret agents. Law and justice, they were for us Norwegians yours and mine and our neighbors' ideas of our responsibilities toward each other and our rights which we would not permit to be violated, put into words by spokesmen whom we ourselves had elected, enforced by a machinery of justice which had authority because we had commissioned it to act on our behalf. So it had always been in Norway, with back-slidings and interruptions, since ancient times, when peasants and kings met in *things* to talk together and formulate the laws of the land." With law our country shall be built, and not with lawlessness destroyed," begins one of the oldest documents in Norwegian history which we possess, the Frostating Law. Can it surprise anyone that we hate with full and passionate hearts the strangers who now destroy with lawlessness the country which we have built up with law through thousands of years?

We have been systematically plundered by the Germans, we have learned that they steal like crows. We have always known that our country was relatively poor in natural wealth. But we had learned by experience that it is possible to live quite well in a poor country if industry, forethought, reciprocal helpfulness enter into the effort to make the most possible out of all sources of livelihood. Our state economy was, accordingly, a thoughtfully developed, fine, and sensitive mechanism; after a year of German power it has practically gone to rack and ruin. In international scientific co-operation we uphold our honorable place; now the strangers work brutally and with conscious purpose to transform our entire system of education, from the elementary schools to the university, into a system of which the goal is not to enlighten but to obscure. Superstition and fables, party political "science" are to be crammed down Norwegians, small and large, by right-believing Nazis and their Norwegian servants.

What the Norwegians feel toward the vice-government of Quisling and his liege vassals, which could not exist for twenty-four hours if German military might did not protect it, was expressed by a young Norwegian boy, escaped from occupied Norway this winter, in this way: "It feels as if the oppressors were holding us down and smearing us with our own excrements."

Can anyone wonder that we hate the aggressors? Or that we think with fearful forebodings of the future – no matter how firmly we believe that some day our country will again be ours? When we know we must build again from the ground all we had created in the last hundred years or more, with the soul of the people poisoned and embittered by the barren passion which hatred is.

2

That was Norway. Does anyone believe that the hatred is less in Poland? In Yugoslavia? In Greece? In Italy? In England? Do the Americans themselves know how they will feel the day Germany's designs against the United States are fully revealed – all the undermining they have carried on in this country, the full extent of the Nazi's hatred of all the ideals and institutions which constitute America's stake in world culture and the eternal honor of the American people?

What Frenchmen really feel toward Germany today is a thing apart. France has been defeated before now, the French people have been toppled down into bottomless misery and suffering before now. Not once, but many times before, Paris has been in the hands of foreign forces; the Parisians, helpless, have had to endure humiliations and pillage at the hands of an army of occupation. But never before has it been required of the French people that they should themselves mock and deny their past, condemn their own creative genius as a phenomenon of degeneration, surrender their souls and let themselves by animated by the glorious German national soul. Miranda, ravished by Caliban, must not only stand ready to do his will, she must be forced to declare she loves him, looks up to him, that she will gladly cease being Miranda and be Caliban's image, his obedient, fawning little helpmate.

"It is undoubtedly so, in spite of all talk of individual good or bad in individual Englishmen, Frenchmen, or Germans, that now during the war we tend to personify every country. We conceive of the souls of nations as individuals, personalities.

"I try to remember impressions of Germanism

which have affected me as something beautiful or good. Landscapes, city scenes with something miniature-like in their beauty – the spirit of delightful children's books. I remember from art galleries faces from a vanished time: their beauty was in their quiet. I remember little verses which with finished grace express the soul's faint vegetative movements. Always something which turns the thoughts to Snow White, who sleeps in the glass coffin somewhere in among the low German mountains. But – a violent movement, a gesture, a strong outbreak of feeling – and all becomes ugly, clumsy, false, and ridiculous. While France – it is beautiful movement, of the soul and of the body, – like the French landscape where heaven and light and haze gather all details into a unity which is grand, festive.

"It seems to me unthinkable that the German people will ever give up their militarism willingly, no matter what it costs them. I wonder if the German people do not need militarism as the lobster needs its shell – the hard exterior an armor enclosing a soft, boneless body. For Prussianism's harsh discipline, Prussian administration, are certainly essential to the life of a Greater Germany – the shell which gives strength and locomotive power to a people whose innermost structure is soft and spineless.

"But therefore it is not envy or rancor, not even fear, first and foremost, that rouses those who look with horror at Germany's advance. It is mankind's instinctive partisanship for that which has its strength, its backbone, within, and a soft, sensitive skin toward the world, in its fight against the giant crab's odious claws.

"One finds deep and hidden meaning in the smallest things. Marika Stiernstedt has placed the woman who sows of the French stamps as a vignette in her book. One remembers Germania on the German stamps – with her helmet on her head and two more helmets on her breasts; the very source of mother's milk has been encased. And one looks at the sowing woman; how free and unprotected she carries her beautiful body in her airy garment, how elastic and light of foot she moves forward against the wind and casts her seed!

"Yes, she is a fitting representative of France's soul, and no one can preserve his soul's neutrality who believes she is fighting for her life against the ugly baggage from *Siegessäule*, she who wants to endow the world with her shells and teach it to move so automatically and grotesquely.

"But the soul of France has done just this, has sowed fruitful seed at all times. In the history of Europe the soul of France has been like the good fairy godmother in the fairy-tales, and the world will be dreadful if the fairy godmother is vanquished."

This is something I wrote in the summer of 1918, in a review of a Swedish book, *The Soul of France*, by Marika Stiernstedt. It is possible that I should not have been able to express myself so soberly about the soul of Germany if at that time I had been able to imagine that not twenty-five years later the giant crab's claws would clutch all Europe, including my own fatherland. And the soul of France – God help it. For my misgiving would appear to be sound: The German people did not give up their militarism. And willingly they will surely never do so.

The power and glory of the Hohenzollerns passed away, – the last Kaiser of the glorious royal house made his inglorious sortie. And we who had known Germany before the first World War – with almost touched astonishment had been witnesses of the average German's pious worship of a Kaiser whom the rest of the world agreed in finding a little comical, however differently one judged William II's personality in other respects – we could not really imagine what the Germans would do now. Gone were all the small kings, all the royal houses, all the resplendent uniforms which had rejoiced the hearts and minds and eyes of Germany's higher and lower middle classes every time they were treated to an exhibition of court life and military parades.

I remember an elderly soldier who had been at the front: he was a little disabled and seemed completely nervous; he was our guide in one of the small palaces in Nymphenburg in the spring of 1925. All the while he led my mother and me through the gilded rococo rooms, he talked convulsively about the vanished Bavarian royal house, to which he evidently rendered almost godlike worship, entirely disregarding the fact that the unfortunate house of Wittelsbach had for generations been ravaged by insanity. "We Germans cannot live without lords whom we look up to," burst out of him, while the tears gushed from his eyes. My mother and I mumbled some sympathetic words, while we tried to get away from him, deeply embarrassed as we Scandinavian people become when we are forced to be witnesses of German *Gefühls-Exibitionismus* (exhibitionism of emotions). Anders – he was twelve years old then – crept back of my skirts, his face as red as a peony with shame.

No single note in the ingenious play upon the deepest strings of the German people's souls which Adolf Hitler has carried on is more ingenious than precisely this: that he has demanded to be worshipped as a godlike being. Thereby he met a German need since time immemorial, a need which was already the chief motif in the German medieval poems about the Niebelungs' tragic fate, the yearning for an unconditional subjection under a master. There *could* have been something beautiful in this faithful servant ideal, if it had not had a wrong side which is also clearly apparent in the Niebelung legends: loyalty to a lord and leader justifies every crime, every lie, every act of treason which the sworn servant performs against others – if he only believes, or can persuade himself to believe, that it is in the service of his lord that he makes himself a villain.

Besides its wrong side, this idea also has a

supplement, which makes it even more repellent in the eyes of most non-German people. To the need of feeling a master's foot on his neck corresponds a need for having someone under him, on whom he himself can trample. If any of us were among the doubters, when Hermann Rauschning in *The Revolution of Nihilism* quoted Hitler's pronouncement that this was his life's purpose as Führer: to realize this German ideal on a hitherto unknown scale, we have now seen myth become fact. If Germany is able to dictate a new world peace, it will create a new social order – with a German master people, arranged in a pyramid, descending from the godlike Führer figure at the top, in steps of overlords, middle-lords, and under-lords. And beneath the feet of the under-lords the conquered peoples who are to be the helots and slaves of the Germans. However inconceivable such an ideal seems to, for example, us Norwegian people, who literally feel as great an aversion to trampling on a living being as to being trampled upon, at least as long as we are normal, this social plan must nevertheless appeal to something in the mentality of the average German. In this closely packed *Volkheit*, which under oppression from above will get the right to oppress those below, individuals will be released not only from every duty, but also from every possibility of taking up an independent attitude – a possibility and a duty which again presuppose that the individual has a backbone and that his organs of equilibrium are in order.

It is a well-known fact that practically the entire body of Europe's folk-lore – the orally transmitted treasure of folk-legends, myths, fairy-tales, and ballads – is the common possession of all its peoples; much of this folk-lore has been replanted in American soil from all corners of the Old World. Not a few of these folk-tales have emigrated to Europe from Asia, not a few of them have parallels and kindred forms in the Negroes' and Indians' treasure of folk-lore. But there is a German folk-legend which has never been told by any other people, as far as I know; that is the legend about the Pied Pier of Hamlin. It is exclusively through printed sources that this legend has become known outside Germany. That is, the first part of the story is known also from other parts of the world: in Norway and Denmark, for example, we have a legend about a stranger who comes and offers to free a district from the vermin who infest it – swarms of rats or (in Norwegian and Danish forms of the legend) a deluge of vipers. Now, it is a common feature in all folk-lore – legends or fairy-tales – that animals act and behave and talk as if they had human minds. Michael Fox and Bruin in our Norwegian folk-tales, coyotes and buffaloes in the prairie Indians' stories, seals and white fish in Eskimo myths, tigers and jackals and apes in Hindu fairy-tales, have been endowed with human mentality. But to confer rat mentality upon their own children, to invent a story in which human children, small girls and boys, react no differently from any other swarm of vermin – that the Germans have been alone in doing. The story about the Pied Piper of Hamlin is so intimately German that it must seem completely incomprehensible to all other peoples. It is the most subtle and revealing self-portrait that any nation in the world has ever produced.

For this let nobody imagine that Hitlerism represents anything new, an alien ideology, which has been injected into the veins of people sucked empty and bled white by the cruel and wicked Versailles Peace. (The harsh dictates of the Versailles Peace were discarded one by one by the victorious nations, who in the first place had no over-supply of common interests and mutual confidence, and in the second place suffered from a common bad conscience. Both in England and in America it was contrary to all the emotional tendencies of the common man to deal justly rather than mercifully with a defeated opponent.) Moreover, of course, certain well-to-do circles in the victorious nations were haunted by a delusion (if delusion is not too pretty a name for wishful thinking) that German Nazism and Italian Fascism meant a bulwark against Russian Communism, which they, with some justice, feared more than the devil himself – although they had ceased to believe in the devil, in personified but bodiless, superhuman, crafty evil. That Nazism and Fascism were at least equally irreconcilable opponents of

Christianity, and far more perfidious enemies of all the ideals in which, to a certain degree, they still believed and which they served in word, and partly also in deed – that they were constitutionally unable to understand.

Nazi Germany's peculiarities – in the character of the people, in life aims and ways of life and in national ideals – are not anything new. Quite the opposite: they have been traits in the psychology of the German people since time immemorial, which Nazism has brought into the full light of day, and to which it has done homage as the characteristics of a master race – static traits which are responsible for the fact that Germans have changed astonishingly little in the last thousand years. And those elements within the German people which were potentially able to tow the genuine, backward German people a distance forward toward contemporary western European customs and concepts are probably now completely eliminated – exiled or tortured to death in concentration camps and prisons.

The oldest history of Denmark was written just before the year 1176 by Svend Aggesön, a Danish nobleman and nephew of an archbishop, who saw to that the boy received the best education of the time in a monastery and (pretty certainly) studied in Paris some years as a man. Svend did not, however, choose to take orders; he was a military leader and landed proprietor. But his bookish interests and his considerable narrative talent he revealed in his little history of Denmark, told in good Latin and with an unusual feeling for dramatic and lively depiction. About one of the first conflicts between the Danes and their powerful neighbors in the south, Svend tells how the King of the Danes, Vermund, had grown old, weak, and blind. His son, Uffe, was considered incapable, stupid, and half-witted. (Vermund and Uffe belong to prehistoric times.) Svend says now:

"When now the rumor of his weakness had spread itself to the countries on the other side of the Elbe, then the German pride swelled with bloated arrogance, since it never can be satisfied with its own boundaries. And the Kaiser worked himself up to a mad fury against the Danes, when he discovered a prospect of winning a new scepter by conquering the kingdom of the Danes. [As one sees, Svend was no poor psychologist. He would not have been a whit surprised at Hitler's screaming about Polish atrocities and plans for attack against the Germans in the summer of 1939. Svend knew his Pappenheimers.] Imperial messengers were then dispatched, who were to bring the said King of the Danes, Vermund, the haughty prince's commands and give him the choice between two things, neither of which, however, was a good choice. He ordered him, namely, to abdicate his kingdom to the Roman Empire and pay tribute, or to find a warrior who was fit to dispute it in a duel with one of the Emperor's warriors.

"Uffe, the King's son, stands up and declares himself willing to fight the duel against the representative of Germany. And he consoles his countrymen: 'Let us not permit defiant threats to move us. For it is an inborn trait of German arrogance that it must boast with bombastic words, and that it knows how to frighten peaceful and weak people with a whirlwind of threats.'"

Are there any of Germany's neighbors who have not had reason to endorse old Svend Aggesön's characterization of the "Teutons," in the more than eight hundred years that have elapsed since he inscribed it on the parchment?

Some years later Sverre Sigurdsson, one of the most individual and most vital figures who has ever been King of Norway (died 1204), made a speech to the citizens of Bergen about the city's foreign trade. He thanked the English merchants who had come to Norway; the trade with England was all right, for the Englishmen knew how to make it profitable and advantageous for both sides. The trade with Germany, on the other hand, he saw no reason to encourage, because the German merchants wanted only to line their own pockets – take out of Norway the essential products of the fisheries and cattle-breeding, and give the Norwegians in exchange positively harmful luxuries, like German ale and wine. (Sverre is the first temperance speaker we know of in Norway.) Unfortunately, it was not possible for the Norwegians to follow the trade policy he proposed. With the result that the agents in Bergen of the Hanseatic cities tyrannized the city brutally for several hundred years, and made the fishing population in northern Norway poor slaves under the German "office" in Bergen. It is this Hanse rule that the Germans today have impudence enough to tell us was a period rich with blessings for Norwegian economic life, so we should be glad that they have returned to reintroduce similar conditions in Norway.

There was no talk of "Prussians" at the time when Svend Aggesön wrote and Sverre Sigurdsson spoke against German arrogance and greed. The Prussians were then not much more than a wild Slavic tribe which lay and grubbed in the deep forests and bottomless marshes, in the country which was later called East Prussia and Brandenburg. It is of Teutons, Saxons, Germans, that the medieval historians write. It is of the Saxons that a Danish chronicle-writer says (I cannot quote the passage verbatim; I hunted for it in the Royal Library in Stockholm, but did not succeed in finding it, before I had to leave Sweden) that their brutality and braggadocio are boundless, where they have the upper hand, but if luck turns against them, they beg for sympathy and howl like kicked dogs. Is there anyone who doubts that if the Allies succeed in defeating the slave-holding states' attack on all societies of free men in the world, then we shall hear this age-old Teutonic dog-howl rise toward the skies as never before in the history of the world?

O God, save us from denying the Germans our help in freeing themselves from this morass of despair and misery, moral and economic, in which they are already floundering, which will threaten to engulf them completely if they are defeated in this war. For their own sakes, if not for Christian and humanitarian reasons, the victors will be forced to try to put Germany on its feet again economically, as quickly as it can be done, even if it should develop that it is impossible to help Germany, in the first dangerous time after peace has been made, before Germany's victims have been helped. Since all European countries which have been under totalitarian rule, Communistic, Nazi, or Fascist, will be poorer than Lazarus, this task will fall heavily upon America's United States and Latin South America. England may perhaps expect help from its dominions, Holland and Belgium from their overseas colonies, if they succeed in defending them against the plans of the dictator states to grab them and suck them dry. Norway, through its merchant marine, which it saved from Nazi Germany's claws, is earning money and should upon an eventual peace be able to manage, almost without help, since the value of transportation commodities will be raised very much, when we have to rebuild a ruined fatherland. But only the states in the Western Hemisphere will still have the power, if they have the will, to help the worst-suffering countries in the Old World – Poland, France, the Balkan states. But if it should turn out that Germany cannot expect to be helped before Germany's victims have received aid – something which may also take time since means of transportation after the end of this war will be sadly depleted, as a result, among other reasons, of Germany's war at sea – is there anyone who doubts that the German cur-howls for sympathy, for "Help me first even if the situation of my victims is worse than mine," would not swell to heaven in the post-war world?

I am aware that to many Americans, used to hearing about "sweetness and light" and "international goodwill," it must seem completely wicked, and moreover very unwise, that I have said so much about the hatred of Germany and of all things German, though that hatred is a fact, which all plans for the work of reconstruction after this war, and all efforts to create an internationally more just and better order between nations, will be forced to take into account.

Actually, I think that Americans should be quite well qualified to understand that such a hatred is a reality which it is impossible to disregard. Do not the Americans themselves have dearly bought experiences of how difficult it has been to conquer that bitterness which the War between the States here in America left behind? Are its aftermaths completely overcome even today, when it must be clear to all Americans, that if the Union had not been re-established – at a frightful price – then it is likely that the divorce between the Northern States and the Southern States would have been followed by new separations between states with conflicting interests, and by new wars between states and combinations of states within the territory which is now America's United States? Do not Americans know the bottomless depth of bitterness the Irish people feel toward England, as do also many of the descendants of Irish immigrants to the United States? The blackest leaf in England's history, the crimes against Ireland, is certainly not forgotten even now, and it would not be human if Ireland had forgotten it. But it seems inconceivable to an outsider that today there are still Irish who talk as if they could wish England's downfall – now when every sensible person must be able to see that today a victory for England and its allies is the only thing which can save Eire's newly won and dearly bought independence, save it from new slavery, under new masters, who are oppressors by principle, and according to carefully devised methods – a people which would never tolerate that its victims should find allies among the ruling people, that any Germans in Germany should raise their voices in advocacy of the cause of the subjugated people, even if it should happen that at some time a generation of Germans might arise which could conceive of justice as not exclusively that which serves the selfish interests of Germany. No matter how incomprehensible it may seem to a Catholic from Europe, one sometimes gets the impression that even Catholic Americans of Irish descent, descendants of men and women who heroically endured suffering and persecution for the sake of their faith, do not see what Nazi Germany's victory would mean for the fate of the Catholic Church in the world. The Pope is today, practically speaking, a prisoner in the hands of a power which has never concealed that it hates Christ, that one of its aims is to eradicate Christianity and make its own morality of violence a new religion. There are surely not many European Catholics who doubt that one of the first things we should see after Germany's ultimate victory would be a drama the like of which the world has not experienced since ancient times: that of a pope condemned to a martyr's death on trumped-up charges. And a phenomenon which Christianity has not seen since the Middle Ages: that German rulers now, as they used to do then, setting up a rival pope and creating a new schism within the Church, which it could take centuries to overcome.

3

In Europe, at any rate, we had in the most recent past – the past which ended when this war broke out – accustomed ourselves to regarding people as economically determined beings. The assumption was that social progress from ancient times to our days was determined by economic problems, in times of both war and peace. But in the same way our forefathers, from the Renaissance period on to the full flowering of nationalistic ideas, regarded men as politically determined beings; the battle down through the ages had always centered on freedom for social groups and individuals, the rights and freedoms of citizens. In the same way the people of the Middle Ages thought of themselves as souls, beings which could never cease existing; whatever else they could or could not do, extinction was denied them, in eternity, amen. Life here on earth was the decisive moment in our eternal life, in which we had to choose between a future in bliss or in torment. All conflict was at bottom conflict between faith which led to salvation and faith which must lead to perdition.

Each of these points of view had, of course, led men to a discovery of something fundamental in their own nature: We fight to explain away the soul's existence. We fight for our fate in all eternity also when we try to prove that there is no life after bodily death. We fight as political beings even when we fight to become political minors, to rid ourselves of all individual civic responsibility and to be allowed to hide ourselves in a *Volkheit* or a proletariat, or another form of the masses or classes. And we have also always fought about economic values, for our real or imagined economic interest – to improve our living-conditions, or to prevent others from improving their living-conditions at our expense.

But in just these last decades before the outbreak of this war we were making some additional discoveries about our own human nature: that our psychic life is influenced to a much greater degree than we formerly had suspected by psychological factors. Our bodily health or sickness is influenced by the soil on which our house stands, by the water which we drink, by the food we eat, by the harmonious or discordant relations with the people we live with. And that health or sickness in our psychic life is, to a much higher degree than we had dreamed, determined by our physiological condition. And all conflict between human beings is also a strife between healthy and sick souls.

There is one thing which psychopaths cannot possibly do: that is to establish a peaceful and satisfactory relation to their fellow men. Psychopaths are constitutionally unpeaceful, spiteful, obsessed by grudges against real or imagined antagonists. That is to say, in reality, every single person with whom they come into more than the most passing contact.

The gifted psychopath has again and again in the course of history found the solution for his hostile attitude toward man – as war lord or revolutionary. As he gives himself up to the dream of a future when the community, or men, or his nation, or his "race," or his social class, shall have developed itself into something entirely different from what it is today, the psychopath can also imagine that there is something human which he does not hate and stand outside of. If not any single person, then at least his own imaginary picture of a mankind which can never be materialized in his lifetime, which will never demand the impossible of him – that is, that he shall adapt himself to life with other people. In that way the gifted psychopath escapes from having to admit the truth – saves himself from having to admit, he cannot be the friend of any person, nor feel such universal human symptoms of psychic health as compassion, sympathy, friendship, understanding of other people, but is condemned by a hard physical necessity to waste his love on dogs and cats, to weep his tears of sympathy over a dead canary, or a handful of frozen violets, as Martin Luther says that he did.

It does not mean that one underestimates the significance which economic conditions have had in the development in Germany, both in the more distant past and in the period between the two World Wars, if one points out that this development is conditioned by the many psychopathic characteristics which can be traced in the German psyche as far back as the Middle Ages. Epidemics of mental disorders, which other peoples, seemingly at any rate, have outgrown, seem today to lie latent in the German people. Anti-Semitism, for example, is surely no exclusively German phenomenon. But that the mentality from the days of witch-baiting and witch-persecutions could appear again in any other civilized people as we have seen it in the German persecutions of the Jews, that is indeed difficult to believe. In so far as it is possible to place any confidence in the accounts that are made public through the newspapers and radio of the German occupied countries, it appears that France, where there was assuredly before the war much anti-

Semitism of a peculiar French type – and Italy, where as far as I know there was no anti-Semitism worth mentioning – are only very reluctantly adopting the persecution of and injustice toward their Jewish populations along the lines decreed by the German lords of these countries, out of their hysteria and wholly paranoiac hatred of Jews.

Even in the thought-movements which are essentially the products of German minds, and which are Germany's most important contributions to the European culture milieu – the Reformation and romanticism – both schizophrenic and maniac-depressive traits are predominant. Luther was a psychopath, and so were most of the German Reformation's "heroes," in so far as they were not syphilitics in far advanced stages of the disease. Psychopaths, suicides, fanatic ego-worshippers, wild dreamers, and tuberculosis patients, with the heightened self-absorption of sickness, were the majority of the great poets whose names are synonymous with German romanticism's artistic conquests; for it is true that the threat of destruction of personality in insanity or death very often stimulates gifted individuals to heightened productivity. It literally looks as if such a threat, of early death or madness, is necessary before German talents can be stimulated to produce something above sheer mediocrity; while, for example, English genius as often seems to be the fruit of health and normality, intensified to the highest degree.

While it has always seemed to Germany's

neighboring peoples as if the German concepts of honor were little developed – that is to say, that they know relatively little of our concepts of uprightness, individual responsibility in relation to other people, veracity, and spiritual reserve and modesty, self-control in behavior, all that makes up our ideals of conduct for men and women in life – Germans have always had their own concepts of honor, linked to death and destruction.

I remember what a terrifying impression it made on me, in my young days, when I was the secretary at A.E.G., Berlin's Norwegian branch, and in the way of business, so to speak, I had as one of my tasks each morning to read through the day's issue of the *Berliner Tageblatt.* There were constantly recurring notices of child suicide, a phenomenon which I had never heard tell of from any other place. Pupils who cannot adjust themselves in school, failures in examinations, adolescent difficulties, children's tragic fight to gain a foothold in the world of adults – all such things one knows well from all parents of the world. But that large numbers of children give up the fight, that such things can drive, not a single child, but innumerable children to take their lives, that has at least until now seemed unthinkable to everyone except the Germans.

Duel morality and its accompanying rules regarding situations in which a man of honor must commit suicide, child suicide, suicide epidemics, which recur again and again in Germany's cultural history, are significant complements of German militarism. At one time we were inclined to place the entire blame for militarism, with all its terminology of the mailed first and blood and iron and Germany's unsheathed sword which pointed now here, now there, wherever German territorial expansion might be desirable, on the junkers and nobility, the princes and the vociferous Kaiser William II. Junker militarism has been succeeded by an even more fanatic and ruthlessly destructive militarism, supported from its beginning by the upper and lower middle classes of Germany. And I am certain that if, for example, a new revolution in Germany should within a year and a day make Nazi Germany a Communistic or proletarian Germany, then the German people would still seek their way of life in a renewed and aggressive militarism.

One thing is certain: Hitler's plan for establishing a new social order in Europe will never be accomplished, even if he should succeed in crushing every single country which still bears aloft the old European standard, of faith that the goals toward which it is worth while to work are: free citizens, the right of the individual to his honor and his dignity and to private human happiness so long as he does not seek it at the expense of others. Militarism has never shown constructive force. And the German people have shown little ability as social builders. The sustaining forces in the fields in which Germany really has contributed to Europe's cultural heritage, in free research, scientific work, and to a certain degree in art (although Germany's contributions in fields other than music have rarely been first class) – they are now subjugated or driven into exile or they are perishing in concentration camps. In the tracks of a victorious Germany will follow economic and cultural ruin in every country on which Germany lays her mailed first. And Germany will be forced to make even more strenuous efforts in the fields which have consumed all the creative ability, all the constructive imagination of the people – invention of new weapons, new methods of war. So the giant crab, when it has sucked its victims in Europe to skin and bone, can stretch out its claws for booty on other continents.

4

In her book *Mission to the North* Mrs. Florence Jaffray Harriman has a sad little epitaph for the International Exhibition of Polar Exploration, which was to have been opened in Bergen in the summer of 1940: "Not the least anguishing part of this war is, that it tore to tatters and postponed for years, though certainly not for ever, so many enterprises that were international and humane – so much fun, so much sharing of science, so much practical hope for linked progress of all nations."

It is plain to everyone that a victory for the dictator states will mean that this scientific collaboration will be stifled for an indefinite time. It is on the program of the totalitarian states that science is to be abolished; for no matter how much one gives the name of science to the work of a staff of state servants who have been ordered to manufacture more or less plausible explanations and excuses for the tyrants' whims and caprices, that kind of activity can never achieve any similarity to science worth mentioning. And so intimate has the interrelation between all forms of scientific research become that if the right to free inquiry is abolished in one or several fields, it will profit little if the totalitarian states still encourage scientific work in fields which they think have food value – as the basis for technical advances or improved agriculture, for example. In the scientific world it is now more important than ever that one works for all, and all for one. Moreover, it is clear that the subjugated peoples would not be encouraged to make any scientific contributions, no matter how able they have shown themselves when they had their freedom. Consider Germany's treatment of its Jewish scientists, her planned assassination of science in Poland, Czechoslovakia, Norway.

Victory of the democracies is the essential basis for any resumption of international scientific collaboration within a future not entirely beyond our range of vision. And our hope that the devastations of this war may be repaired within a surveyable future is to a vital degree linked with the belief that this international scientific collaboration can be resumed, and the certainty that it must be resumed on a scale never before known.

This must, of course, be done with a full recognition that science is something different from what the masses imagined – at least in Europe before the war. "It has been scientifically proved," people used to say about whatever theory their favorite newspaper or magazines or popular primers advocated. Rumors about scientists' experiments or working hypotheses were circulated in this way in the broad classes of men and women, who had absorbed the knowledge a standardized school system manages to impart to children before adolescence sets in and the child's natural curiosity must be second to the young person's interest in self. The endless work, the sum of hypotheses and experiments which it always costs to attain anything which resembles certainty, results which are substantial enough so anything further can be built upon them, common laymen now also are beginning, perhaps, to understand a little. No human beings are infallible, scientists no more than other people. But they have, often at any rate, to a greater degree than other people the cardinal virtue called patience.

Patience is a maligned virtue, perhaps because it is the most difficult of all virtues to practice. It has been slandered, distorted, represented as something negative: the placid submission of the wronged and suffering to ruthless oppression and evil fate. It is in reality the virtue which has made it possible for man to win most of the lasting values he has achieved in this world: the courage to turn back when one sees that the way one has chosen does not lead to the chosen goal, but toward something else. The courage to begin again, when one's plans have suffered shipwreck, the courage to seek a solution for the tasks one has set for oneself, even though after any number of attempts they seem insoluble. Surely nobody will deny that the people who have gone through the hell of this World War will be as unfit as men can be to practice patience or even hear talk of patience. If nothing else, we know it from the experience of the former World War. That is why I believe that this time the men who are to find the ways out of the mire and to lead the war-ravaged nations out of the ruined cities, bring back to health all that can be saved of a spiritually and physically broken-down people, and undernourished, bewildered children, must take the scientists into their counsels in quite another way than politicians and leaders of the people ever before have been willing to do. Whatever forms the new league of independent nations will take, equally necessary as organs for common defense and economic cooperation will be organs for common permanent scientific collaboration, and these must be given power and authority quite different from what his hitherto been granted the experts whom various governments have used in various fields.

Not least where the problem of Germany is concerned. It will be useless to go on believing that there is no fundamental difference between the

German people's nature and the nature of all other European nations. We must not go on believing that our inability to understands the Germans, and the Germans' inability to understand all peoples other than themselves, are only a difference in degree; they are not essentially different from the lack of understanding that has so far characterized the relations between people with different historic assumptions and different types of civilization. A small stratum of the German people – with freer and more receptive minds than the masses, with more ability to digest information (to procure information was not difficult in pre-war Germany, the difficulty was that the masses interpreted everything they learned in their peculiar way), with more curiosity about other people's actions and thoughts – felt themselves members of the common European cultural circle and acted accordingly. But that stratum was thin – in fact, only a film on top of the soup kettle. The great German people stood outside it, or, more accurately, they sat outside it. And when they arose it was to undertake marauding expeditions into the alien – all that was not Germany.

That was how it could happen that though hosts of German scholars in the course of time have made their honorable contributions in all fields within the international world of scholarship, German universities could produce and harbor professors who thought and wrote like Messrs. Treitschke, Banse, and the whole company which has blossomed forth in the last decade, after the majority of honest and genuinely scientifically thinking Germans had been outlawed or buried in inactivity, poverty, or concentration camps. That is now it could happen that a poet like Friedrich Schiller, who made himself the spokesman in Germany for his period's longing for freedom from all kinds of tyranny, for freedom of thought, and political freedom, could be worshipped as one of the nation's great names without the masses of the people being in the slightest degree contaminated by his desire for freedom and his revolutionary spirit; there simply was not fertile soil for that kind of ideas in the deep strata of Germans. That was how it could happen that though German diplomats, German nobles, German officers, met members of their own classes throughout Europe and associated with them as equals, the German officers could, at home, assert their superiority over the civil population in a way which in every other place in the world would be considered downright gross and boorish. That was what made it impossible for us, in my youth, really to understand German girls of the same age: they could not fall in love without exalting their feelings to the skies and raving about being won and conquered (in practice, of course, they had their artful little methods of captivating and taming their heroes). We could not understand that they thought that whatever wore a uniform was manly and glorious that a man with his face hacked with dueling scars was not unappetizing – quite the contrary.

It will be necessary for historians, ethnographers, and ethnologists, but first and foremost doctors and alienists, to devote to the problem of Germany the most intense study – and in part on a new basis. The new co-operation between historical science and pathography, between state experts in economics and psychiatrists, will perhaps bring the understanding, which alone can help to overcome the hatred of the Germans – if people can become convinced that the mass of the Germans "knew not what they did," when they gave in to the manic-depressive and paranoiac elements in their nature and again and again flocked around a man who stood up and offered to lead them, or sought their leaders, *because* they were psychopaths. The German people are obviously no "race" (not even the result of the meeting of fairly pure racial elements and the mixture of racial residues on central European soil). But they are an ethnic group, a human stuff which has lived under the same historically and environmentally determined conditions, an endless number of families intermingled through legitimate and illegitimate sexual relations; and it seems that unhealthy and fatal racial heritages have riddled the entire ethnic group to a higher degree than elsewhere.

They themselves have, of course, wanted to pose as "Nordic people," on the basis of the fact that Germany in ancient times was inhabited, in addition to Celtic, Slavic, and Alpine tribes, by a number of tribes which were latter called Germanic. Because the population of the Scandinavian countries also have Germanic tribes as forefathers, the Germans have tried to persuade themselves – and us – that we are "racial kinsmen," and that this professed family relationship should make it easy and natural for them and us to understand each other. It is possible that their most recent experiences in Norway and Denmark have taught all parties that is was a mistake. It is nearly two thousand years since their and our "Germanic" racial ancestors parted company for good, and long before that time many of the tribes had settled permanently in widely separated regions of Europe;. Historians figure an average of three generations to a century (in older times there actually were four or five generations in such a period). We and the Germans would then be something like cousins forty times removed. Nobody can expect that the family resemblance should still be striking. – That approximately one per cent of Norway's population in spite of this have felt that the Germans were their racial kinsmen, and have enthusiastically offered themselves for co-operation with them – and that this one per cent consists largely of pychopaths and cranks, people who have been punished for crimes of various kinds, and misfits who had no chances to satisfy their ambitions in a society where law and order and decency prevailed – may be a fact which psychologists and psychiatrists will study with profit.

The Germanic tribes were, however, not a Nordic people. Originally they probably emigrated from the mountain regions and plateaus of central and southwestern Asia. The tribes which have also been called Goths settled along the North Sea coast and the coast of the Baltic Sea and *became* Nordic people. The proximity to the ocean, the necessity of seeking their livelihood on the ocean, molded their nature, perhaps more than any other factor. It is not strange that we and the Germans are as different in nature as nations on the whole can become.

For it is not impossible, perhaps, that in spite of everything it is the Germanic elements in the German compound of peoples that have most determined its natural quality. The Germanic tribes in what is now Germany lived in dark, swampy forests, along marshy river banks. But for wild primitive peoples (as the Germans were when they came to their later dwelling-places in Europe) the forest is terrifying, full of secret and mysterious horrors – not like the ocean, a harsh but honorable enemy and an open-handed friend. In the forest the single individual is lost; the horror of the forest squeezes courage and manhood out of the solitary man. To succeed against the forest he must join with many, be one in a group. The mentality of the horde, the cruelty which always rises in a horde, because each separate individual in the horde has a half-conscious sense of his lost manhood which he must avenge, and his irresponsibility which he wishes to enjoy, are, of course, not a peculiarly German phenomenon. But nowhere else in the so-called civilized world do psychologists and psychopathologists have so immense and fruitful a field as here for study of the nature of mass mentality, its destroying and decimating power in human society. Here the Pied Piper from Hamlin or Hell has his eternal hunting-ground. The ancient and rockbound German faith in that "ruthlessness," refined cruelty, and terror is a patent method by which to attain all the winnings and benefits for which a horde of irresponsible individuals can wish, is perhaps an inheritance from the forest-terrified old "Germans," and likewise the dream of breaking out of the forest prison and conquering the homesteads of other people and the fruits of others' work, rather than trying to transform their own homeland into a freeman's society – a dream which has taken form in the shifting communities and creation of ephemeral states of the folk-migration periods, in the attempts of small German kingdoms to conquer and subdue one another during the Middle Ages and the time of the Reformation, in *Drang nach Osten* and *Drang nach Westen,* in the Hohenzollern conquest politics from the days of Frederick the Great to those of William II, in the enthusiastic adherence of German youth to the highly un-Nordic Adolf Hitler's promises to the German people of world rule and unlimited plunder.

It must now be the business of ethnographers and ethnologists, but first and foremost of doctors and psychiatrists from the whole world, to try to get to the bottom of the factors – racial inheritance, physical constitution, means of subsistence, education, customs and habits, soil and climatic conditions, which together have created what today is called *Deutschtum.* The significance of such research work on German human materials would among other things be an invaluable aid to the understanding of reactionary and destructive forces in all people who impede the forward march toward more secure and free conditions within all nations. By these means the relatively new discipline which is called social mental hygiene could surely make enormous gains.

Not that I think the doctors are infallible any more than other people, or that the fundamental happiness and welfare of mankind will be assured even if medical science should be able to prevent paranoiacs, infantile egoists, manic-depressive psychopaths, sexual invalids, day-dreamers incapable of fellow-feeling and of working with their fellow men as equals, from getting the opportunity to run amuck unhindered in society and work evil on a large scale. But if it becomes possible to diagnose Hitlers, Görings, and Goebbelses while they are still very young, place them under medical care, or isolate them if they are incurable, then certainly much unhappiness could be prevented. Doctors and alienists would thus gain a large field of activity in the affairs of society.

We have during the last generation heard an uncanny amount of talk about what people expect of the future in the fulfillment of some "dream" or other. The real conquests which men have achieved down through the ages they have not dreamed into existence. The ideals of democracy have never been dream pictures, but goals. There is nothing dreamy about the men who took the fate of the American colonies in their hands and risked the life and welfare of these same colonies in an attempt, which succeeded quite well, to give them the freedom which they believed the colonies needed. They were not infallible, they were of highly variable moral quality, these founding fathers of the United States – but dreamers God knows they were not. Nor were our Norwegian "Fathers from Eidsvoll" dreamers – the men who hazarded Norway's welfare in the fight for Norway's existence as an independent kingdom, who gave Norway the freest constitution any country in Europe at that time had ventured to build its future upon. We, who count ourselves their spiritual descendants, will also be forced to decide, after careful deliberation, on which roads we shall go forward toward our and our forefathers' goals. We shall need courage, and far-sightedness, the will to fight against obstacles, to achieve them. We shall need courage, courage, and more courage. Courage to meet difficulties, courage to conquer scorn of all moral idealism, which can so easily cut a sad figure in a world where moral honor and greatness are so rare and difficult, moral hypocrisy the easiest way to evade the demands of morality. Courage to meet difficulties and courage to bear success – so we do not settle down, if we are successful in anything, never after even the most glorious victories believe that now the battle is won for good and always. Let us finally never imagine that any "wave of the future" will ever carry us toward any goal. The way forward toward our goals we will find only through our own exertions, through tireless, patient, and courageous exertion.

Order Form

Name_____

Address_____

City_____State_____Zip Code_____

Phone Number _____

E-mail Address_____

#_____ Return to the Future Copies @ $13.95 each   Subtotal $_____

Minnesota residents add
6.5% sales tax on book only   Tax $_____

Plus Postage and Handling
$4.50 for the first book plus
$1 for each additional book   Shipping $_____

                                                 Total $_____

We accept checks, money orders, Visa or Mastercard
Visa/Mastercard Number _____

Expires _____

Signature_____

Send all orders to:
Scandinavian Marketplace
P.O. Box 274
Hastings, MN 55033-0274

Or call us at 800.797.4319

Or visit us on-line to place orders or seek additional information:
www.scandinavianmarket.com.